Better Homes and Gardens®
SCRAP
CRAFTS

Credits

Better Homes and Gardens® Books
Editor: Gerald M. Knox
Art Director: Ernest Shelton
Managing Editor: David A. Kirchner

Crafts Editor: Nancy Lindemeyer
Crafts Books Editor: Joan Cravens
Associate Crafts Books Editors: Debra Felton, Laura Holtorf,
   James A. Williams

Associate Art Directors: Linda Ford, Neoma Alt West,
   Randall Yontz
Copy and Production Editors: Marsha Jahns, Nancy Nowiszewski,
   Mary Helen Schiltz, David A. Walsh
Assistant Art Directors: Harijs Priekulis, Tom Wegner
Senior Graphic Designers: Alisann Dixon, Lynda Haupert, Lyne Neymeyer
Graphic Designers: Mike Burns, Mike Eagleton, Deb Miner, Stan Sams,
   D. Greg Thompson, Darla Whipple, Paul Zimmerman

Editor in Chief: Neil Kuehnl
Group Editorial Services Director: Duane Gregg

General Manager: Fred Stines
Director of Publishing: Robert B. Nelson
Director of Retail Marketing: Jamie Martin
Director of Direct Marketing: Arthur Heydendael

Scrap Crafts
Crafts Editors: Joan Cravens, Debra Felton, Laura Holtorf,
   James A. Williams
Contributing Crafts Editor: Ciba Vaughan
Copy and Production Editor: Mary Helen Schiltz
Graphic Designer: Lynda Haupert

Introduction

Wonderful things from bits and pieces—that's what scrap crafting is all about. As you use this book, you'll be delighted to discover the hundreds of imaginative projects you can make for yourself, your loved ones, and your home using materials you already have on hand. Whether your collection includes fabric and lace, leather leftovers or chunks of wood, pretty papers, or postage stamps, you're sure to find just the project to suit your skills and your supply of scraps.

Contents

Dolls and Toys from Odds and Ends

Children love handmade toys, even when they cost almost nothing to make. So shop here for a baker's dozen of whimsical dolls and other playthings to craft from clothespins, wooden spoons, slivers of fabric, leftover lumber, tin cans, and cardboard. You're sure to find at least one that's perfect for your favorite child.

Pennywise Projects for Your Home

Crafters everywhere will appreciate these good-looking home furnishings and accessories. Choose from quilts, pictures, tablecloths, lamps, rugs, afghans, and kitchen accessories to make quickly and easily using wood, paper, yarn, fabric scraps, and other materials you may already have on hand.

Craft Your Own Christmas Cheer

The best Christmas ever at your house can begin with an inexpensive supply of vintage neckties, last year's wrappings and holiday cards, dabs of paint, or bits of rope and muslin. Craft these exciting trims (plus lots more), or knit surplus yarns into a patchwork afghan bedecked with all the festive symbols of the season.

Glossary

Design and Photography Credits

Index

Collectors and Savers

What nicer way to begin our book than with projects that make the most of a scrap crafter's treasures? Whether you are a serious collector or simply a devoted—and thrifty—saver of things you like, you're sure to find some ideas in this chapter to spark your creativity and inspire you to show off your collection in new and imaginative ways.

Like the stamp-studded desk accessories at left, most of these projects call for a large supply of one sort of scrap (labels or lace, printed T-shirts, or fruit and vegetable seeds, among others). But the scale of a project can always be adjusted to suit the size of your own collection. A quilt design adapts easily to a crib-size throw, for example, and a single nosegay of dyed seed flowers retains all the charm of the more bountiful bouquets on page 18.

For instructions for the stamp projects, please turn the page.

Stamp and Label Projects

"Stamped" Desk Accessories

If you don't have a cache of stamps, hobby centers and stamp shops often sell bags of stamps for a small sum.

To remove stamps from envelopes, soak the corner in lukewarm water for several minutes until the stamp slides off. Dry stamps on newspapers and press them between books to keep them flat.

───HOW TO───

Materials
Assorted stamps
White glue, rubber cement, spray adhesive
Clear acrylic spray
Cardboard mat frame, hexagonal wooden planter, small boxes, note cards, tin can, scraps of wood, key chains
Wood stain
Scraps of cardboard and print wrapping paper
Scissors, craft knife

Instructions
• **Picture frame:** Using rubber cement, glue stamps to the frame. Coat with clear acrylic spray.

Now cut a piece of cardboard ½ inch smaller than the frame; cover it with print wrapping paper. Spread white glue inside the edge of this backing piece, along the bottom, and up two sides. Press in place on back of frame, leaving top open for insertion of photograph.

To make an easel stand, cut a cardboard strip 1½ inches wide and three-fourths the height of the frame, then cover it with print wrapping paper. Bend under the top inch of the strip and glue this piece to the back of the frame, positioning the strip to support the frame at a slight angle.

• **Planter:** Stain inside and top edges of container; let dry. Coat with clear acrylic spray. Glue stamps to outside of planter with white glue diluted with water. Trim stamps flush with top and bottom edges of the container and finish with several coats of acrylic spray.
• **Pencil and brush holder:** Affix stamps to metal can with diluted white glue; trim edges. Add a stripe of gold paint to top and bottom rims; finish with acrylic spray.
• **Note cards and gift boxes:** Glue stamps to squares, rectangles, or colored paper, then glue these "framed pictures" to purchased note cards or to the tops of small, paper-covered boxes.
• **Key chains:** Drill a hole in a small scrap of wood. Sand, stain, and seal with acrylic. Glue stamp to center of wood piece; embellish with paint. Coat with clear acrylic spray. Add a chain.

Cut-and-Paste Kitchen Tricks

Colorful pictures of fruits and vegetables clipped from labels—or gathered from seed packets and a host of other sources—add country charm to these accessories.

To remove labels from cans or jars, soak containers in warm, sudsy water for 10 to 20 minutes. Gently peel off labels, pat dry with newspaper, and weight with a heavy object to keep flat until dry.

───HOW TO───

Materials
Pictures of fruit, vegetables, and other motifs
Dark green poster board
Clear, adhesive-backed plastic
Scraps of felt for backing

Wooden tray (removable back)
Glass storage jars
Ringbound scrapbook with
  "peel-and-stick" pages
White typing-weight paper
Press-on letters (optional)
White glue, rubber cement
Acrylic spray

Instructions

• **Coasters:** Glue fruit or vegetable pictures to centers of 5-inch squares of green poster board; cover each with a slightly larger square of clear, adhesive-backed plastic. Back each with felt.

• **Trivets:** Arrange four small label pictures on a 10-inch square of poster board and glue into place with rubber cement. Finish as for coasters, above.

• **Tray:** Cut a piece of poster board to size, glue a selection of motifs in place, cover with adhesive-backed plastic (or glass from the tray), and insert in the tray. Secure with small finishing nails, if necessary.

• **Storage jars:** Glue pictures of fruits or vegetables to the fronts of assorted clear glass storage jars as "pictorial labels" for home-canned contents. Protect labels with clear acrylic spray (the labels can then be wiped clean, but will not be totally waterproof).

• **Illustrated cook book:** To embellish a collector's album of your (or a friend's) recipes, use decals and clever paper cutouts. First, copy your recipes onto clean white paper. Then add funny titles and spruce up the margins with appropriate illustrations. It doesn't matter if you're not much of an artist—just let the cutouts do the work. And if your printing isn't up to par, rely on press-on letters to spell out the information. Slip each recipe sheet into a peel-back, plastic-covered page to keep it safe from kitchen splatters.

Cut a piece of paper to size for the cover and decorate it in a suitably personal fashion. Glue sheet to cover of book, and protect with clear, adhesive-backed plastic.

Handkerchief Treasures

What a great way to show off a collection of vintage hankies! If you have an extensive collection, fashion a fabric of floral hankies to drape on your bed. Or, if you've only one or two hankies, create pillows with lots of store-bought laces, ribbons, and trims for a romantic addition to your bedroom.

Hankie Coverlet

HOW TO

Materials
48 (or more) vintage or
   dime-store hankies
2 flat sheets to fit your bed
Quilt batting
Sewing threads in various
   colors, straight pins

Instructions
Preshrink and iron hankies and sheets before you begin. Then, lay one sheet on the floor or atop a large flat surface. Smooth out quilt batting, then lay the other sheet on top so the batting is sandwiched between the sheets.

Arrange the hankies on the top sheet, striving for a pleasing balance of colors and patterns. Allow the edges to overlap slightly so that none of the sheet is exposed. Hankies with special details (such as a single large flower) or fancy embroidered edges should overlap straight- or plain-edged hankies.

When the arrangement is satisfactory, pin the hankies in place, making sure the pins go through the batting to catch the bottom sheet. Sew around each of the hankies with matching threads to anchor the hankies and quilt the coverlet at the same time.

Finish the edges by turning in a 1-inch hem all around. Or, finish with a shaped hem by stitching around the edges of the hankies and carefully cutting away any excess sheet.

Handkerchief Pillows

HOW TO

Materials
12-inch square embroidered or
   appliquéd handkerchief for
   each pillow
½ yard of cotton fabric in white
   or a color to complement
   hankie for each pillow
½ yard of polyester quilt
   batting for each pillow
Polyester fiberfill
Pregathered eyelet, lace, other
   trims, and ribbons

Instructions
Cut fabric into two 14½-inch squares. Baste handkerchief to the center of one of the fabric squares.

Add laces, trims, and ribbons to pillow top. Sew on pregathered lace or eyelet around the outside edge of pillow top.

Cut two 14½-inch squares of batting and baste one of these to the wrong side of the pillow top. Baste the second square to the wrong side of the second fabric square (the pillow back).

Place pillow front and back together with right sides facing. Pin the outside ruffle to the inside to avoid getting it caught in the seam.

Using ¼-inch seams, sew pillow together leaving a large opening along one side. Then, to square up the corners after the pillow is turned right side out, stitch across the corners, ¼ inch inside the angle of the seams.

Turn pillow right side out and stuff firmly with fiberfill. Blindstitch the opening closed.

New Uses for Old Doilies

Almost every needlework aficionado has a dainty doily or two stashed away. Too beautiful to toss and too delicate (or dated) to use, they stay in a drawer, waiting to be rescued.

Now's the time to retrieve those treasures and try out one of the charming display ideas shown here. If you think Aunt Mary's antimacassar is a real work of art, then show it off in a frame that says so. Or, tack your collection of crocheted beauties to solid-colored throw pillows for an almost-instant touch of Victoriana.

Stained or damaged doilies recycle into one-of-a-kind mats for wonderful old family photographs. And if you can't find frames to flatter your doilies, just make your own from lightly stained and mitered strips of decorative molding.

Framed Doily

HOW TO

Materials
Special doily
Two sheets of 1/8-inch-thick acrylic plastic
4 clear acrylic screws
Monofilament (fishing line)

Instructions
Have plastic sheets cut to size (at least 2 inches larger than height and width of doily). Then ask the plastics studio to drill 1/4-inch-diameter holes in each corner of the two sheets (lining up holes) with a special drill bit (to avoid cracking the plastic).

Secure doily to one sheet of plastic with tiny dabs of white glue. Allow glue to dry thoroughly, then add the second sheet of plastic

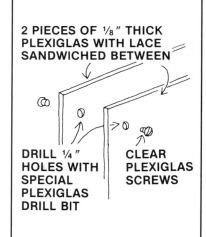

2 PIECES OF 1/8" THICK PLEXIGLAS WITH LACE SANDWICHED BETWEEN

DRILL 1/4" HOLES WITH SPECIAL PLEXIGLAS DRILL BIT

CLEAR PLEXIGLAS SCREWS

and slip in clear screws. Before tightening screws, slip clear monofilament line around each of the top two screws and tie off. Tighten screws; hang picture in a window.

If you prefer, hang lace between two sheets of glass in a conventional wooden or metal frame. Or, back lace with a contrasting piece of fabric, then frame and hang.

Doily Pillows

HOW TO

Materials
Crocheted or other lacy doilies
Collection of solid-colored, purchased pillows (or fabric and polyester fiberfill)

Instructions
One of the simplest—and most striking—ways to show off a collection of old lace doilies is to tack them to the front of a collection of throw pillows. Whether you start with purchased pillows or make ones in sizes that suit your supply of doilies, use tiny hidden whipstitches to secure the lace pieces to the pillow tops.

Doily Picture Mats

==========HOW TO==========

Materials
Assorted doilies
Medium-weight poster board
Spray adhesive, white glue
Scraps of cotton fabric
Craft knife, picture frame

Instructions

First, cut a piece of poster board to match each doily. Then cut a round or oval opening in the center of each mat. Spray mat with adhesive and smooth doily in place. (If doily is lacy or has cutouts, cover mat with contrasting fabric first.)

Cut out center of doily to within ½ inch of edge of mat opening. Clip, fold, and glue fabric to back of board. Edge each opening with bias-cut fabric strip, if desired. Add picture and insert mat in frame.

T-Shirt Pillows

Sentimental attachments are the source of the one-of-a-kind collection of T-shirt pillows shown above. Here are plump, pleasant reminders of summer vacations, favorite cities, football teams, and social causes—even the foods you love! You might stitch and stuff a set of pillows to celebrate all of your favorite things, or concentrate on a single theme, like sporting events or vacation spots.

════HOW TO════

Materials
Assorted printed T-shirts
Polyester fiberfill

Instructions

To make a pillow, turn T-shirt inside out and stitch across sleeves and bottom. Run a second line of stitching ¼ inch inside seam, for added durability. Trim away excess fabric, turn pillow rightside out, and stuff with fiberfill. Slip-stitch neck closed.

Many T-shirts, particularly large-size ones, will make more appealing pillows if stitched into shapes somewhat smaller than the actual size of the shirt—that is, shorter and narrower. Study the pillows in the photograph, above, for suggested shapes and proportions.

For a round pillow, cut off the shirt sleeves, turn the shirt inside out, and sew from shoulder to shoulder in a wide U shape. Turn, stuff, and stitch the neck closed.

Old-Clothes Quilt

What could be more comforting than to stitch up a kid-pleasing quilt from a collection of out-grown (but well-loved) clothes? This oldie-but-goodie quilt is as quick to make as it is inexpensive. Simply clean out the kids' clothes closet and set to patching!

HOW TO

Materials
Two twin-size sheets
Matching quilt batting
Assorted, out-grown clothes in medium-weight fabrics
4 yards of coordinated fabric for binding
Embroidery floss

Instructions
To begin, cut the pieces of clothing into workable-size patches. Stitch the patches to a twin-size sheet in a random pattern, overlapping the pieces and turning under raw edges where necessary. Work with single layers of fabric, clipping away zippers and heavy seams wherever possible. Stitch patches in place, and add touches of embroidery, if desired.

Next, back the quilt top with batting and a backing sheet. Tie the three layers together, and bind the edges with 6-inch-wide strips of coordinated fabric.

Label and Patch Projects

To collect the small appliqué blocks for the box and belt shown at right, raid the closets with a small pair of sharp scissors in hand. Carefully clip labels from clothing, trim edges, and remove any loose threads. Wash labels in warm water and gentle suds, if necessary. Pat them dry between towels and press lightly on the wrong side.

Label Sewing Box

HOW TO

Materials
Sturdy cardboard box with
　loose-fitting top
Assorted clothing labels
¼ yard each muslin, batting,
　and fusible webbing
Lightweight cardboard
Print fabric for lining
Red thread, white glue

Instructions
　Trace outline of the box top on muslin and cut out, adding an inch margin on all sides. Cut a matching piece of fusible webbing and baste to the muslin piece.

　Arrange labels on the webbing side of this muslin cover; butt edges of labels up against each other without overlapping. Using a press cloth, fuse labels in place. Fill seams between labels with ¼-inch-wide machine satin stitching in red thread. Press on wrong side.

　Cut a piece of batting to fit box top; glue into place. Stretch the label-appliquéd fabric over the top; pleat, pin, and blindstitch at corners. Pull seam allowance to inside of top and glue into place.

　For sides of box, cut muslin as wide as the height of the box and as long as the circumference of the box—adding 1 inch on all sides. Baste a piece of fusible webbing to one side of the muslin.

　Arrange labels on fusible webbing; press into place. Satin stitch between labels as before; press on wrong side. Stretch strip around box; blindstitch at corner. Pull seam allowance to inside and bottom of box; glue into place.

　Cut cardboard to fit inside sides and bottom of box. Cover each piece with batting, then cover with print fabric; glue edges of fabric to back of cardboard. Glue these lining pieces inside box. Repeat for box top.

Label Belt

HOW TO

Materials
2½-inch-wide belt backing
　equal to circumference of
　waist plus 4 inches

Fusible webbing, lining fabric
Purchased belt buckle
Assorted labels, red thread

Instructions
　Baste a strip of fusible webbing to belt backing. Cover the first 1½ inches of one end with backing fabric; this end will be wrapped around the belt shank. Cover remainder of belt with labels, butted edge to edge. Shape the other end to a slight point and trim labels to fit. Press all labels into place.

　Machine-sew ¼-inch-wide satin stitching between labels, but do not stitch along edges of belt. Next, cut backing fabric to size and press into place with fusible webbing. Again, satin-stitch around edge of belt. Trim backing fabric, if necessary; repeat stitching. Attach buckle to squared-off end of belt.

Stitch a colorful quilt to show-case your child's collection of sports letters and souvenir patches. Or, if the collection is still at the Little League level, patch a pillow for starters.

Sports Patch Bedspread

========HOW TO========

Materials
Assorted patches
Two twin-size sheets (or equiv-alent fabric)
Matching sheet of batting
Scraps of fabric in assorted solid colors
Fusible webbing (optional)
Kraft paper

Instructions
On kraft paper, draw eight 20-inch squares. Arrange 15 to 20 different patches on each square. Next, divide each large square into smaller squares and rectangles to frame each patch. Number the squares and their corresponding patches for easy assembly.

Use paper patterns to cut out squares and rectangles of solid-color fabrics to serve as back-grounds for patches (add ½-inch seam allowances). Sew small squares and rectangles together to form a large square. Then center patches on their respective back-ground pieces, secure with fusible webbing, and slip-stitch in place.

Repeat for all eight squares. Then join the squares with 4-inch-wide sashes of sheeting or solid-color fabric and add 12-inch-wide borders on all four sides.

Pin and baste batting between pieced top and backing sheet. Hand- or machine-quilt as desired, then bind edges of quilt with matching bias strips.

18

Seed Flowers

A splash of dye and a dab of glue turn ordinary fruit and vegetable seeds into an imaginative and glorious bouquet of everlasting blossoms.

Collect seeds after your family meals. Or, if you're in a hurry to "grow" your own seed flowers, simply pick up a generous assortment of fruit and vegetable seed packets from a local garden shop.

HOW TO

Materials
Assorted seeds (sunflower, squash, apple, grapefruit, cantaloupe, tomato seeds, plus cherrystones and other small fruit pits)
Liquid fabric dyes in assorted colors
Small stainless steel or enamel saucepans
Green poster board
White or tinted card stock
No. 24 green florist wire
Green florist tape
White glue
Clear acrylic spray
Tweezers, darning needle

Instructions
Wash and dry all seeds thoroughly to prevent mold. Sort seeds according to type and store them in airtight jars or other containers until they are ready to use.

Use seeds in their natural state, without dyeing, or color them with fabric dyes. To color seeds, mix just enough dye in boiling water to color the seeds you plan to use. Add seeds to dye bath and simmer over a low flame until they reach the desired shade. Rinse seeds in cool water until water runs clear, then dry them on newspaper.

To create a flower, first cut a quarter-size circle from green poster board to use for the flower base. Make two holes, about 1/8 inch apart, in the center of the circle with a darning needle. Insert one end of a piece of florist wire into one of the holes, bend a hook in the wire and feed the end of the wire through the other hole. Twist ends of wire together on the back side of the cardboard, then wrap wire stem with florist tape.

Cover the top of the flower base with a thin layer of white glue. Let glue dry until tacky.

Beginning on the outer rim of the cardboard circle, place seeds side by side around the base, using tweezers to maneuver the seeds into the desired position. Continue adding the seeds by working in a circle around the edge of the base, then moving in toward the center. Add more glue as necessary. A single cherry pit or a cluster of tomato seeds makes an attractive center on flowers.

When all the seeds are in place, set flowers aside in a container to dry. When dry, spray flowers with several coats of clear acrylic.

For small cards and gift tags, glue the seeds directly onto small, folded pieces of card stock. Simple flower designs work best for the cards—those with only a single row of petals and a single seed or small fruit pit for the center. You may wish to add a tiny sprig of dried grass or leaf just below the flower to make the arrangement more graceful.

Collector's Display Table

What nicer or more attractive way to show off your collection than in this 36-inch-square coffee table? We've included directions for making the table as shown, but you can easily adjust the size of the "boxes" to fit your own special cache of collectibles.

HOW TO

Materials
9 feet of 1x12-inch clear pine
12 feet of ½x3-inch pine
12 feet of 1x2-inch pine
4x8 feet of ¾-inch birch plywood
Birch plywood edging
34½-inch square of ¼-inch plate glass with beveled edges
Sandpaper; stain, varnish or Danish oil

Instructions

For the sides of the display table, cut four 15x36-inch pieces of birch plywood, mitering the edges of the 15-inch sides. To make the table legs, on one long side of each piece, center and cut out a 2x24-inch section as shown in the diagram at right.

Nail and glue together the sides of the table; clamp until glue is dry. Then cover all end grain of the plywood with birch edging strips.

Next, cut ½x3-inch pine into four pieces, each approximately 34¼ inches long, to fit the inside dimensions of the table. (Measure *actual* dimensions before cutting the pieces.)

Butting the ends of the pine strips against each other in the corners, nail and glue the pine strips to the inner sides of the table ¼ inch below the top edges of the sides. These cleats will support the glass tabletop.

From remaining birch plywood, cut a 35-inch-square "floor" for the display area (see diagram below). Mount the plywood beneath the ½-inch-wide cleats that will support the glass by turning the table upside down and resting the plywood square atop the ends of the pine strips.

Next, to support the "floor," cut 1x2-inch pine cleats. Each one should measure approximately 34¼ inches long, but measure the actual dimensions for your table before cutting the strips.

Nail and glue these cleats into place (butt-joining the ends) as shown in the diagram. When dry, turn the table right side up again.

To make the dividers, cut the 1x12-inch clear pine as follows: First, rip the length of the 1x12s into strips 2⅞ inches wide. Then, cut eight dividers, each 33½ inches long. Next, stand each divider on edge and rip the narrow (¾-inch) edge in half, making 16 pieces, each measuring approximately ¼x2⅞x33½ inches. Sand the dividers smooth, using a belt sander if possible.

Next, cut notches in the dividers. To ensure the identical placement of notches in all strips, clamp the strips together and simultaneously cut notches in all of them using a table saw.

Place notches as follows: Mark the exact center of the strip with a pencil; then measure and mark notches 3 inches on each side of the center, then 5 inches from the notch just marked (on each side of the center), then 2½ inches from the notch just marked, and again 2½ inches from the notch just marked.

Cut notches halfway through the dividers so they are measured on center. Width of notches should equal width of strips.

To assemble the partitions, position eight strips with the unnotched edge next to the "floor" of the table. Then insert the remaining eight strips into the first ones so that the edges interlock.

To finish the table, sand all surfaces smooth. Stain and varnish or treat with Danish oil. When dry, fill spaces with your collection and lay glass on top.

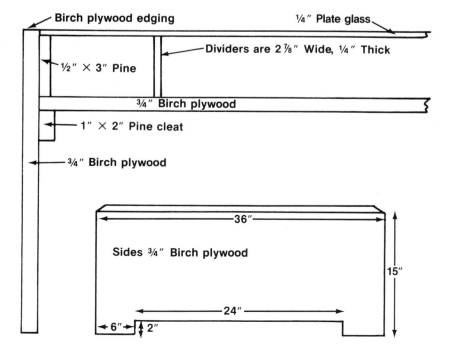

Birch plywood edging — ¼" Plate glass

Dividers are 2⅞" Wide, ¼" Thick

½" × 3" Pine

¾" Birch plywood

1" × 2" Pine cleat

¾" Birch plywood

Sides ¾" Birch plywood

36"

15"

24"

6" — 2"

MAKE THE MOST OF

Bits and Pieces

Tiny though they may be, some scraps are still too special to toss. Whether it's a pretty flower salvaged from an old postcard, snippets of floss in a favorite color, or scraps of wood and odd-lot nails, the devoted scrap crafter just knows that someday these small treasures will come in handy.

To hasten that day, we've put together an intriguing assortment of small but spectacular projects that use a minimum of materials for maximum effect.

The turn-of-the-century-style trinkets pictured here are a case in point. For complete instructions for making these brooches and baubles, the sweet-smelling sachet hats, and the tiny treasure boxes, please turn the page.

Turn-of-the-Century Trinkets

Picture-Hat Sachets

These sweet-smelling hats are an enchanting Victorian way to scent a drawer or freshen a closet. You might also stuff one or two with a mixture of fiberfill and emery powder to use as pincushions—they make lovely gifts (and unusual Christmas ornaments, too)!

HOW TO

Materials
6-inch-diameter white straw picture hats (available in craft and hobby stores)
Acrylic paints
Narrow lace and gold-toned ribbon
⅜-inch-wide satin ribbons
Small fabric leaves and purchased flower stamens
White glue
Scraps of print fabric
Potpourri, sachet, or emery powder; fiberfill

Instructions

Paint the underside and outside of each hat in the colors of your choice (we used Aquatec/Bocour iridescent colors). Line each hat with a fabric pouch stuffed with potpourri, sachet powder, or emery mixed with fiberfill as follows:

First cut a 5-inch-diameter circle of lightweight cotton fabric. Gather the edges of the circle and stuff it with a small piece of fiberfill and one tablespoon of potpourri, sachet powder, or emery. Draw up the gathering stitches around the circle, making a bag, and fit the bag into the crown of the hat, with raw edges tucked inside.

Stitch the bag in place, sewing through the straw (trim on the outside of the hat will cover stitches).

Arrange lace trim and gold ribbon around the crown of the hat as a hatband; glue in place. Cut 10 inches of gold ribbon, fold into a loop for hanging, and tack ends to hatband at center back. Cover raw edges and seams with a bow made of matching ribbon.

For flowers (about 7 for each hat), gather 5 inches of ⅜-inch-wide satin ribbon into a rosette and tie off. Insert several pearl flower stamens through center of each flower and glue the stamens in place. Clip ends; let dry. Glue flowers around front of hatband. Cut 1-inch-long leaves from larger leaves; glue around each flower.

Elegant Cards and Gift Boxes

Special wrappings turn even the tiniest gift into a special occasion.

HOW TO

Materials
Card stock
Small gift boxes
Foil and patterned papers
Paper seals and floral or other decorative motifs
Scraps of lace and trim
Spray adhesive, rubber cement
Rubber brayer

Instructions

For gift boxes, give top and bottom of box a light coating of spray adhesive. Cut foil or patterned wrapping paper to size and press in place. Smooth raw edges of paper to inside of top and bottom.

Using rubber cement, decorate the top of each box with a simple collage of seals, stickers, trims, lace, or snippets of paper doilies.

For gift cards, coat a sheet of card stock lightly with spray adhesive. Press foil or patterned gift wrap into place and roll with a brayer to remove all creases and air bubbles.

Cut small gift cards and tags from foil-covered stock and fold in half. Using rubber cement, decorate the front of each card with a collage of cutouts and trims.

Brooches and Buckles

There's no need to raid Grandma's jewelry box for romantic accessories of yesteryear. The antique-look baubles, opposite, are easy to make from an assemblage of floral stickers and decals. Glue them on painted metal forms and slick their tops with a glimmer of gold.

HOW TO

Materials
Copper discs and metal buckle forms (from craft shops) and/or button forms (from notions counters)
Flat white enamel paint
Polyurethane or decoupage varnish
Decals, flowers clipped from wrapping paper, old seals and stickers
White glue, sandpaper, epoxy cement
Gold leaf paint, small brush
Pin backs, purchased belting

Instructions

Sand metal forms lightly, then paint discs, button forms, and belt buckles with two coats of white paint. Dry, seal with varnish, and lightly sand again.

Center decals, paper seals, or cutouts on pins and buckles and secure with a thin coat of diluted white glue. If necessary, clip into edges of decal or cutout to make it lie flat on a curved surface.

Seal with several coats of varnish. Sand lightly with fine sandpaper. Paint a fine gold leaf edge around each pin or buckle. Seal with several more coats of varnish.

With epoxy, glue pin backs to discs. Sew leather or fabric belt through buckle shanks.

Paper Crafts

Decorative, versatile, and inexpensive, paper can be used to embellish a startling variety of surfaces—some of which are illustrated here. And because it is available in a nearly infinite variety of patterns and colors, weights and textures, paper offers a virtual smorgasbord of project possibilities. Whether your mood is contemporary, folkloric, or Victorian, you can execute any of the projects shown at left in a paper patterned to suit your fancy!

Cut and Paste Projects

HOW TO

Materials
Wrapping papers in selected small prints and patterns
Decoupage or nail scissors
White glue, brushes
Water-base varnish
Glass bottles, wooden beads, porch spindles or newel posts, and cardboard boxes

Instructions
• **Bottles:** Cut decorative paper into strips; taper strips into blade-like shapes to fit contours of bottle. Dilute white glue with water to the consistency of light cream. Brush glue onto the bottle, then apply paper cutouts. While glue is still wet, wipe off the excess with a damp paper towel. Protect with varnish or polyurethane.
• **Candlesticks:** Sand spindles and newel posts, then seal with diluted white glue. Let glue dry, paint desired areas with acrylics, then cut and glue paper to sections of the posts. Trim edges with a razor blade, if necessary. Hammer a nail into the center of each candlestick; nip the head with metal clippers and file off rough edges. Finish with varnish or polyurethane.
• **Beads:** Sand beads, coat with diluted white glue, and apply narrow strips of paper. Strips should wrap around beads and extend into holes on either end. Smooth wrinkles with thumbnail. Varnish.
• **Boxes:** Cover both tops and bottoms of boxes with paper, then embellish tops with cutouts from cards, old seals, ribbon, and lace.

Picture-This Pins

HOW TO

Materials
Small pictures, prints, stamps, decals, and labels
Construction paper
Water-base decoupage finish
Small paintbrush
Clear acrylic spray
Pin backs, glue
Emery board
Single-edge razor blade

Instructions
Cut each picture to the desired size, adding ⅛ inch on all sides. Cut 5 pieces of construction paper for each picture, making the pieces ¼ inch larger on each side than the picture.

Join the pieces of construction paper together one layer at a time, using a thin coat of decoupage finish between each layer. Press the layers smooth.

Cover the back of the picture with a thin coat of decoupage finish and center it atop the layered construction paper. Gently smooth out any air bubbles and wipe off excess finish. Let the pins dry overnight, weighting each one with a book to prevent warping.

Trim each side with a single-edge razor blade and smooth the edges with an emery board. Spray with clear acrylic and glue a pin back to each one.

Wrapping-Paper Pictures

Here is a novel way to recycle your prettiest gift wraps. We've used a selection of colorful wrapping paper motifs to create these delightful, three-dimensional pictures.

The size of your pictures will depend on the size of the motifs and the number of repeats on the paper you decide to use. With 4-inch-square designs like those pictured, you can make half a dozen pictures from a single sheet of wrap!

HOW TO

Materials
Wrapping paper (four copies of each design)
Cardboard for background
Decoupage or nail scissors
Clear silicone cement and rubber cement
Decoupage or 3-D glaze (available in craft stores)
Glaze thinner; brushes

Instructions

Select wrapping papers with clean-lined designs, such as the floral prints used to make the pictures shown here. You needn't limit your design selection to florals—animals, stylized landscapes, and other motifs are equally suitable. Just remember that you will need four copies—or repeats—of the same motif for each finished picture.

From wrapping paper, cut out three of the motifs, separating the design elements and cutting away the backgrounds. Leave the fourth design uncut.

To begin, use rubber cement to glue the uncut design to a square of cardboard cut to the same size as the print. Next, dab small globules of clear silicone cement on the face of the motif (see photo, right). Let the glue dry until just tacky, then carefully position correspond-

ing segments of the second print atop the dabs of glue. Do *not* press down; just let the print sit atop the glue until dry. Repeat the process two more times, stacking the motifs to achieve the desired three-dimensional effect.

For a more natural, rounded look, roll the edges of leaves and flower petals around a pencil, curling them slightly before setting them in place atop the glue.

When the design is complete, brush on a coat or two of decoupage glaze (thinned, if necessary). When glaze has dried thoroughly, frame the pictures appropriately. Look for fairly deep frames to complement and contain the 3-D effect of the pictures. Once the designs

are framed, these make perfect take-home mementos of a special get-together.

When you've mastered the simple techniques described above, you might want to experiment with larger wrapping paper patterns. Or use inexpensive posters or prints to create an out-of-the-ordinary wall hanging.

Carefully build up the picture, working from the background to the foreground. When working with a larger surface, vary the number of layers used on portions of the picture to achieve greater sculptural relief. For example, you might use only one or two layers for "middleground" areas and build to three or even four layers for foreground details.

Working with Paper

Paper can be folded, cut, and crumpled; woven, twisted, and torn; curled or scored; and colored, printed, embossed, and embellished in hundreds of ways. It comes in an almost infinite variety of colors, weights, and textures, and it's widely available for pennies a sheet.

This incredible versatility—at such a modest price—makes paper one of the most enduringly popular craft materials.

By developing a working knowledge of the most common kinds of paper and of the basic tools and techniques for working with papers, you will be able to take full advantage of this material's exciting potential as a creative medium.

Tools and Equipment for Paper

One of the reasons paper is such a popular craft medium is that the tools you need are often right at your fingertips. Because you are already familiar with the operation of these ordinary supplies, it takes just a few moments to learn how to use them to their best advantage for paper crafts.

Scissors: If possible, keep both large and small pairs of sharp scissors on hand for paper crafts. Large scissors are effective for straight cuts and large shapes, but cannot handle the delicate, precision cuts required for smaller projects. Nail or decoupage scissors with curved blades are useful for cutouts and decoupage work.

Blades: A single-edged razor blade or a craft or utility knife is the ideal tool for cutting long, straight edges or for scoring heavy papers and cardboards. The knives and replaceable blades are available at craft stores. Change the blades often so your cuts will be precise.

Workboard: Cutting or scoring papers with razors or knives is easiest against a workboard of soft wood (such as pine)—but scraps of linoleum, cardboard, or newspapers folded into a pad work equally well.

Measuring devices: A metal-edged ruler, found at craft stores, is essential for most paper crafts. And those old math-class standbys—the protractor, triangle, and compass—are also invaluable for measuring geometric shapes and marking angles.

Miscellaneous: A dime store is a gold mine of paper crafting tools. Pick up a set of tweezers to use for lifting and positioning small pieces of paper. And equip yourself with a simple hole punch—you'll use it in endless ways.

Staplers, of course, are ideal for holding paper together. But consider using paper clips, clothespins, masking tape—even metal hair clips—to hold certain shapes together while glue dries, or while you are assembling other portions of a project.

Adhesives to Use with Paper

Select glues carefully, with an eye to the purpose for which they are intended. The wrong glue can damage a paper project beyond repair. Avoid watery pastes and glues whenever possible—they tend to discolor papers and shrink and distort surfaces as they dry.

Rubber cement is probably the best all-purpose adhesive for most paper projects. It dries quickly into a thin, transparent film, and any excess easily can be rubbed away with your finger.

White craft glues are strong and effective, but they should be used sparingly, in small dots when possible. If applied too heavily or in thick blobs, they will soak through the paper or leave unsightly lumps when they dry.

White glue is useful for bonding paper to other materials, such as wood, glass, or metal. Also, when diluted with water in a half-and-half solution, it is an effective fixative for applying decoupage cutouts to almost any surface, or for making tissue paper collages.

Spray adhesives are as useful for paper crafts as they are for many other craft projects. The two types of spray adhesives available include artist's adhesive, such as Scotch brand Spray Mount®, which is helpful in working out designs that require repositioning the material—such as collages, assemblages, or greeting cards.

This adhesive is clear, quick-drying, non-staining, and allows for repeated manipulation of materials without losing its bonding ability.

The other type of spray is more permanent and quick-bonding, making it useful for gluing larger surfaces together. Both kinds of sprays provide a light, even coating of adhesive that is difficult to achieve with any other kind of glue.

Craft Papers

There are hundreds of different kinds of paper—each with individual characteristics of color, finish, weight, texture, and absorbency that make them suitable (or unsuitable) for specific craft purposes.

A few of the kinds of papers referred to most often in craft instructions are detailed below.

Art papers are high-quality and usually expensive papers that are designed specifically for "fine arts" purposes, such as pen and ink, watercolor, or pastels.

Watercolor paper, for example, has a rough texture that accepts watercolor paint well. It is generally made of 100 percent rag material and will withstand repeated wetting and sponging. Also, it can be stretched on a frame without danger of tearing.

On the other hand, some handmade Japanese papers have an almost blotterlike absorbency and are more appropriate for various printmaking techniques.

Art papers often have exciting textural qualities and can make interesting additions to collages and handcrafted cards. But because they are generally expensive and come only in a pale range of colors, art papers are not appropriate for run-of-the-mill craft projects.

All-purpose craft papers include typing paper, yellow manila paper, and dime-store tablets—all of which are great for roughing out ideas or working up designs.

Kraft paper is a generic term for medium-weight brown wrapping paper, usually sold in rolls, that is popular for packaging, pattern making, and general use.

Newsprint is an inexpensive, off-white paper available in large pads in craft, hobby, and art supply shops. It is somewhat flimsy and not durable, but its large size and low cost make it useful for sketching and for children's crafts.

Construction paper, that old grade-school standby, is a multipurpose, medium-weight paper available in many colors. Usually sold in multicolored packages of medium-size sheets with a matte finish, construction paper is perfect for any number of projects, including cards, decorations, party favors, and collages.

Crepe paper is a lightweight crepe-textured paper sold in rolls or sheets that are available in a huge selection of colors. Crepe paper is extremely flexible, allowing you to pull, roll, and twist it into graceful flowers, ruffled collars, and sturdy macrame ropes. Crepe paper is not particularly durable, but it is inexpensive. Its festive colors make it ideal for an array of party and holiday decorations.

Tissue paper is a lightweight, transparent, and somewhat fragile paper that is available in a decorator range of shades. You'll find it useful for crafting flowers, papier-mâché projects, and collages.

Origami paper is light- to medium-weight and is usually sold in small squares, available in brilliant colors and occasionally in floral prints or foils.

Although thin, origami paper is sturdy and takes creases well. Designed for making folded paper birds, animals, and other objects, it offers a somewhat finer, lighter weight alternative to construction paper for crafts such as Christmas ornaments, collages, and cards.

Its uses are limited by the fact that origami paper is sometimes colored on only one side and is usually available only in small (2-inch to 10-inch squares) sheets.

Gift wraps are specialty papers that add charm and vitality to paper projects. In addition to matte- and enamel-finish papers, look for foil wraps, two-toned and ombré papers, flocked or velour finishes, and motifs that could be used individually in other projects.

Paper Boards

Craft instructions frequently call for various weights of heavier paper or cardboards for making cards, posters, or paper sculptures. Several of the more common boards are listed below.

Bristol board is a high-quality cardboard available in light to heavy weights. Bristol board is smooth, white, and takes paints and inks well. It is also good for paper sculpture.

Oak tag is a lightweight cardboard that is strong, folds without cracking, and comes in a wide range of colors. It's good for posters and paper sculptures.

Poster board, which is available in many colors, is medium-weight to heavy cardboard with a clay-coated surface. It is particularly appropriate for silk screen, pen and ink, and acrylic paint projects such as posters.

Railroad board is a heavier weight cardboard colored on both sides in bright hues. It's useful for posters, cards, and displays.

Foam-core board is a lightweight, yet rigid board composed of a plastic foam core between two smooth paper surfaces. Usually available only in white, it takes color well and is excellent for models, displays, and as a lightweight base for padded fabric projects, such as embroidered pictures.

Paper Potpourri

Some of the most interesting effects in paper crafts are achieved by combining paper seals, labels, stamps, postcards, doilies, and other paper scraps with more conventional paper products. Until you are ready to use them, these materials should be stored flat in boxes and kept in a dry place.

Pretty magazine pictures, ads, and direct-mail materials are often worth preserving for paper craft projects—as are interesting paper shopping bags, foreign language newspapers, and any other scrap of paper that catches your fancy!

Preserving Paper Projects

Although paper is essentially fragile, it can be preserved almost indefinitely with proper care and protection.

For flat surfaces such as collages and cards, several coats of clear acrylic spray or acrylic medium applied with a soft brush will offer adequate protection to designs that are not subjected to constant handling.

For other paper-covered surfaces, you can apply up to 20 coats of a plastic glaze product for strong, durable protection. Plastic glaze is a white, milky liquid that dries strong and clear. Designed for decoupaged surfaces, it also provides a hard, protective finish for papier-mâché pieces.

Two other options for protecting paper-covered projects are clear polyurethane or varnish. If you plan to use either of these products, be sure to select a brand that does not yellow with age.

Finally, whether you frame, varnish, or protect paper projects in any other way, they should always be stored away from excessive heat, moisture, and direct sunlight.

Simple Wood Works

Leftover lumber needn't go to waste—just pick a project to suit the size of your scraps!

Hat and Coat Racks

═══HOW TO═══

Materials
Scraps of ¾-inch pine or other wood
Jigsaw
Dowels
Sandpaper and glue
Varnish or polyurethane

Instructions

Enlarge the patterns, below and right, and trace them onto scraps of ¾-inch pine. Cut out the shapes.

Drill ½-inch-diameter holes as indicated on patterns, holding the drill bit at a slight upward angle. Cut ½-inch dowels into 4-inch-long pieces; insert dowels into holes, securing them with glue.

Sand and finish the racks as desired. To mount the racks, use long wood screws or expansion bolts.

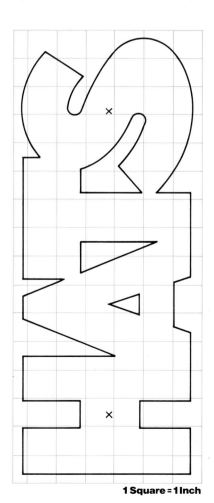

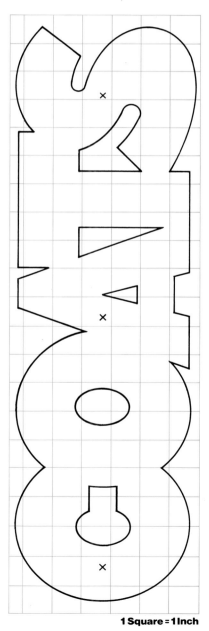

1 Square = 1 Inch

Hardwood Belt Buckles

The full-size pattern, below, and the simple shapes shown on the shelves, opposite, are guides for your belt buckle projects. Experiment with other shapes, sizes, and designs, depending on the wood scraps you have available.

═══HOW TO═══

Materials
Scraps of hardwood (walnut, zebrawood, etc.)
⅛-inch bronze brazing rod (available in hardware stores)
Wood oil, sandpaper

Instructions

Transfer the pattern (or a pattern of your own design) to wood, cut out the shape using a jigsaw, and sand carefully.

Drill ⅛-inch holes through the sides (see dotted lines on pattern). Insert a 1¾-inch piece of ⅛-inch brazing rod through the holes. Bend one end of a 2½-inch piece of rod around the first rod to serve as the buckle hook. To protect the wood, apply an oil finish.

Continued

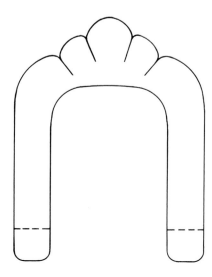

continued

Primitive Wooden Animals

These cheerful, chunky animals (shown on page 34) are constructed of three thicknesses of roughhewn, ¾-inch pine. The pine shapes are held together with wooden dowel pegs and glue.

HOW TO

Materials
Pieces of ¾-inch roughhewn pine
¼-inch and ⅜-inch dowels
Lattice molding for ears
Rattan and rope for tails
Jigsaw, electric drill, belt sander (optional)
Sandpaper, wood glue

Instructions
Enlarge the patterns, right, and trace onto ¾-inch pine. Use a jigsaw to cut out these basic shapes.

Place a belt sander upside down in a vise and sand the outer edges of the shapes (edges that will not be glued together). Round the corners slightly. Or, sand by hand.

To assemble the animals, drill ¼-inch-diameter holes through the body pieces (indicated by the Xs on the patterns). Use glue and ¼-inch dowel pegs cut to fit to hold the pieces together; clamp the pieces until the glue dries.

Use a belt sander or sand by hand to further shape the animals and smooth the edges.

To finish the bull, drill a shallow ¼-inch-diameter hole for the tail and glue a short piece of rope into place. Fray the ends. Drill a ⅜-inch-diameter hole for the horns and insert a 4-inch-long wooden dowel with whittled ends in place.

Finally, drill ¼-inch holes for the eyes and glue whittled scraps of lattice molding in place for the ears (see photograph for placement).

To finish the pig, drill ¼-inch holes for the eyes and two small holes for the snout. Drill a ¼-inch hole for the tail. Soak a piece of rattan in water, wrap it around a dowel, and set it aside to dry. Remove the curled rattan from the dowel and glue the pig's tail in place; trim the end if necessary.

Wooden Rowboat

HOW TO

Materials
Pieces of ¾-inch pine
20-inch strip of lattice molding
Two small screw eyes
Jigsaw, electric drill
Sandpaper, wood glue
Varnish or finishing oil

Instructions
Enlarge the pattern, right, and transfer the boat pattern pieces to the pine board and the two oars to the lattice molding. Use a jigsaw to cut out the number of shapes indicated on the patterns. Sand the edges smooth on all of the pieces.

Glue the five boat pieces together, placing the widest pieces on top. Weight or clamp the pieces together until the glue dries. Cut a 3½-inch-long strip of lattice and sand smooth, then glue it inside the boat for a seat.

To complete the boat, drill ⅛-inch-diameter holes through the oar handles at the dot marked on the pattern. Pry open two screw eyes and thread one hook through each oar handle. Close the openings and mount the screw eyes with oars on either side of the boat.

Seal the wood with varnish or finishing oil.

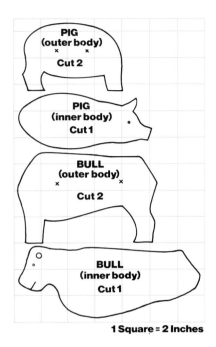

1 Square = 2 Inches

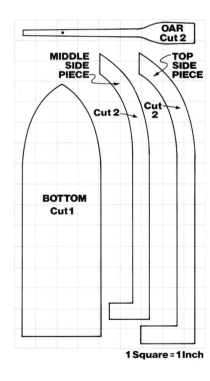

1 Square = 1 Inch

Napkin Rings

Any animal with an appropriately plump shape makes an amusing napkin ring. Experiment with our patterns, then try your own.

──HOW TO──

Instructions

Enlarge the patterns, below, and trace them onto ¾-inch pine or other wood. Cut them out with a jigsaw. (Cut the center hole first, then the outline.)

Drill small holes in each animal for eyes. Sand smooth, then stain and varnish or paint with enamel.

1½"

1½"

1½"

1½"

1 Square = 1 Inch

Wood and Nail Projects

The simple designs, above, are just a sampling of the whimsical wonders you can concoct from odds and ends you will discover in your own workshop. Use these ideas as a point of departure for your own flights of fancy!

──HOW TO──

• **Fish plaque:** Sketch the stylized outline of a fish on a scrap of rough-sawn wood (packing crate or pine scrap—anything will do). Hammer in small nails to outline the fish's snout and mouth, then fill in the body with closely packed carpet tacks to simulate scales. Thread a screw through a washer for the eye and add corrugated fasteners for fins and the tail. Why not design a bird or a very contemporary bouquet of flowers using similar materials?

• **Mini car:** Cut out the basic shape on a jigsaw or whittle it from a scrap of pine. Sand lightly. Drive screws through a set of large and small washers for the wheels, hammer in tiny nails for the headlights and add a heavy-duty staple for the "bumper."

• **Mini horse:** Cut the basic shape on a jigsaw or whittle it out by hand. Add sturdy nails for the legs and a row of staples for the mane, then chip out rough indentations for the eyes.

• **Necklace:** String a collection of cotter pins, nuts, and washers on a leather thong or a piece of polished cord or twine to make a handsome hardware necklace in no time flat. Keep an eye out for other metal oddments to fashion into your own "high tech" jewelry.

Leather Accessories

The luxurious look of leather can be yours for bargain basement prices! Hobby shops are great sources for inexpensive lengths of leather belting and scraps of flexible cowhide to turn into handsome, hand-tooled and custom-dyed accessories like these.

Leather Belts

HOW TO

Materials
Purchased leather belt strips
  (2 to 2½ inches wide)
Buckles and brads
Woodburning tool
Leather dyes, acrylic paints
Small brushes
Spray leather finish

Instructions
Enlarge the patterns and trace them onto belts. Woodburn the edges of the belts, using a metal-edged ruler as a guide to ensure straight lines. Woodburn the outlines of the designs.

For the poppy belt, first dye the background around flower motifs with leather dye. Then paint poppies with acrylic paints thinned to the consistency of light cream. For the butterfly belt, paint motifs with acrylics in colors of your choice.

Protect your designs with several coats of spray-on leather finish. Add buckles.

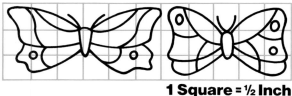

1 Square = ½ Inch

1 Square = 1 Inch

Leather Totes

▬▬▬HOW TO▬▬▬

Materials
Cowhide or other sturdy, flexible leather
Leather dyes, acrylic paints
Small brushes
Wooden mallet, leather tools
Leather finish
Small hole punch, leather laces

Instructions

Select any favorite quilt pattern and sketch the design on clean white paper. Center the paper on a 14- to 16-inch square of leather and trace over the design, indenting the pattern on the leather.

Dampen the leather and keep it dampened as you work. Use a leather knife to lightly incise all pattern lines. If desired, use a mallet and any small, blunt tool to stipple the leather (and add texture) in portions of the design.

Use desired colors to dye the damp leather. Allow dye to dry; apply second coat if necessary. Protect the designs with several coats of waterproof, spray leather finish.

Cut 3-inch-wide strips of leather for sides and bottom of tote. Punch holes and lace pieces together. Add handles.

Cross-Stitch Cards

Odds and ends of linen and floss are all you need to make these fanciful, framable note cards and gift enclosures. With a scant two yards of floss and a couple of inches of fabric (leftover from another project), you can stitch up one of these mini messages in next to no time!

If you're out of floss or fabric altogether, work the same patterns with crewel, tapestry, or needlepoint yarn on mono needlepoint canvas (a #12- or #14-mesh canvas works best). Stitch any word that suits your sentiments—then adjust the size of the cross-stitch border to accommodate your very personal greeting.

HOW TO

Materials

Scraps of #14-count aida cloth or needlepoint canvas
Remnants of cotton embroidery floss in various colors
Embroidery hoop (optional)
Construction paper or colored card stock
Fabric glue

Instructions

If you are working on a fairly large piece of cloth, several greetings may be spaced across the fabric and stitched in an embroidery hoop before cutting them apart. If you have only small scraps of fabric to work with, embroider without a hoop, taking care not to pull the fabric out of shape.

Using three strands of floss, embroider the greeting first, taking each cross-stitch in the letters over one set of threads. Then stitch the border, taking each stitch over two sets of threads. Trim the fabric carefully and fray the edges, as shown opposite.

Cut a 3½x10-inch piece of construction paper or card stock in a color that complements the stitchery; fold it in half to make a 3½x5-inch note card. Apply a dot of fabric glue to each corner of the stitchery and center it on the card. Press the cards between paper towels and weight with books until glue dries.

1 Square = 1 Mesh
Stitch letters over
1 thread and borders
over 2 threads

Pen and Paper Samplers

If you love the look of cross-stitch, but hesitate to take on a long-term project, these short-cut samplers are for you! By simply marking Xs on graph paper with colorful felt-tipped pens, you can capture the timeless beauty of cross-stitch in almost no time flat!

On the following three pages you will find charted patterns for the four examples shown below. But you also can use this simple, color-the-squares technique to reproduce any cross-stitch sampler (or other counted thread design) that catches your fancy.

And here's an added plus: if you are ever tempted to try your hand at cross-stitching the old-fashioned, needle-and-thread way, you'll find that your paper samplers make handy, full-sized, color-keyed patterns for the real thing!

Continued

When I was young
and in my prime.
Here you may see
how I spent my time.

COLOR KEY

1 Square = 1 Cross-stitch

⊞ Pale Green   ◪ Dark Green   ☐ Light Blue   ◉ Dark Blue   ⊟ Light Red   ⊡ Gold   ■ Dark Red

continued

1 Square = 1 Cross-stitch
COLOR KEY   ☒ **Green**   ⊡ **Gold**   ☑ **Orange**   ⧄ **Red**   ☐ **Light Blue**   ◍ **Dark Blue**

HOW TO

Materials
Graph paper (10 squares per inch, available in art supply stores)
Fine-point, felt-tipped pens
Embroidery floss and a fine needle (optional)
Construction paper, mat board, and/or frames
Rubber cement

Instructions

Duplicate the samplers shown on page 42, using the charts on these pages (and on page 43) as a guide. To expand your collection, adapt patterns from cross-stitch samplers found in other books, magazines, or local museums. Try developing your own designs by adapting and recombining traditional cross-stitch motifs, flowers, borders, and verses or alphabets.

Using felt markers in assorted colors, carefully draw Xs in the graph paper squares to re-create the cross-stitch designs. Coloring within the lines counts here: for best results, be sure to mark your Xs neatly from corner to corner in each square.

You may wish to enhance some of the motifs on the finished paper sampler with actual cross-stitch embroidery by stitching through the paper with a single strand of floss. Use an extra-fine needle and be careful not to tear the paper.

Mount the samplers on construction paper to send as very special gifts, or mat and frame them for hanging.

If you're reluctant to tackle an entire sampler at first sitting, reproduce just a portion of one of the designs for the front of a small greeting card. Or give a store-bought clear plastic frame an unexpected, old-fashioned touch: copy the border from one of the samplers and mount it on construction paper to use as a mat for a favorite photograph. You're sure to think of dozens of other uses for these pseudo stitcheries, so pick up your pen and begin!

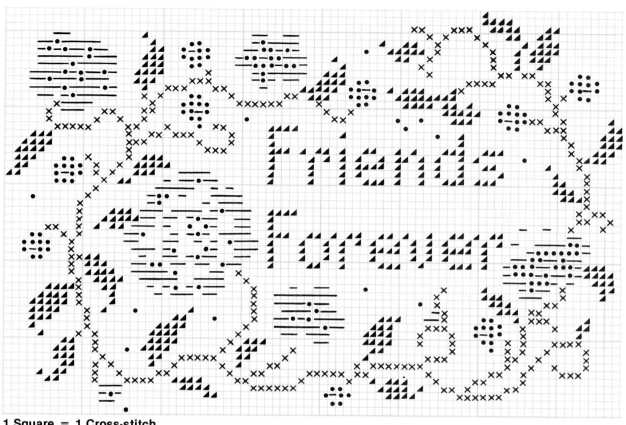

1 Square = 1 Cross-stitch
COLOR KEY ⊠ Green ◢ Dark Green ⊟ Light Red ⊡ Gold

COLOR KEY ⊠ Green ⊡ Gold ⊘ Red ■ Blue   **1 Square = 1 Cross-stitch**

Needle Art Note Cards

Even if you're a novice with a needle, it's a snap to make your own note cards with either one of these crafty techniques.

Pierced Paper Cards

HOW TO

Materials
Glazed or lacquered wrapping papers in assorted colors
Tracing paper
Assorted needles and pins
White card stock
Foam pad, scissors, rubber cement

Instructions
Enlarge the designs, below, and transfer them to tracing paper. Cut the tracing paper pattern and several sheets of wrapping paper to the size and shape of the designs, adding ½-inch margins.

Stack four pieces of wrapping paper and place the traced design on top. (Layer the wrapping paper faceup for a flat design and facedown for a relief effect.) Secure the layers together by sticking pins through the corners of the paper into the foam pad.

Carefully puncture holes in the stack of papers with a needle or pin, following the lines of the traced design. For best results, keep the size of the holes consistent and the pinpricks evenly spaced. If you wish, certain areas of each design can be completely filled in with pinpricks (see heart and bird wings on the card in the foreground).

Next, remove the tracing paper design and separate the papers. Fold cards from the white card stock and cut an opening in the front of each card. Glue the design in place behind the opening, or back the design with a slightly larger piece of contrasting paper and frame it within the opening in the card.

1 Square = 1 Inch

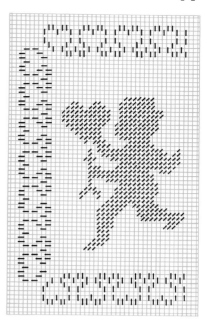

1 square = 1 mesh

Needlepoint Cupid Cards

═══HOW TO═══

Materials
6x8-inch rectangle of #14-count mono needlepoint canvas
Red and white #5 pearl cotton
White card stock
Red foil paper
White glue

Instructions

Following the graphed pattern, above, work the cupid figure in white pearl cotton and the heart in red, using the diagonal tent stitch. Then work the border pattern in white bargello stitches.

Be careful to conceal all loose ends behind the stitched areas, since the background areas will not be filled in and any loose threads will show through the open weave of the canvas. Trim the edges of the canvas evenly.

Cut a 10x16-inch rectangle of card stock and fold it in half. Cut an opening in the front of the card

slightly smaller than the finished size of the needlepoint. Secure the cupid in place with small dabs of white glue. Finally, glue a slightly larger rectangle of red foil paper to the inside front of the card, concealing the raw edges of the canvas. Apply glue only along the edges of the foil paper, and avoid dripping glue on the open meshes of the canvas.

You'll find you can use this same technique to make cards from any simple needlepoint pattern. Just be careful to select designs in which the central motif has a fairly distinct outline, one that does not depend on a filled-in background for effect.

You might also explore working with very small patterns. A single, stylized tulip or a snowflake design, for example, would make a charming motif for a set of gift tags. Experiment with some of the cross-stitch patterns shown on pages 43-45 (a single fir tree, a heart, or a flower) and see how they look when translated onto needlepoint canvas. Successfully combining materials, patterns, and techniques in new and unexpected ways is, after all, the essence of scrap crafts!

Keepsakes

FOR ALL OCCASIONS

Mix imagination, humor, and a sense of the occasion with a modest amount of time and energy and—presto! You can turn even ordinary materials into extraordinary gifts!

For example, why not embroider a "guest book" tablecloth to commemorate a special family gathering? Or craft an elegant "silver" picture frame from dimestore fixings for a couple's 25th wedding anniversary. Or stitch a picture of the "old homestead" for a child going off to college.

Whatever the occasion, a glorious friendship quilt, like the one shown in the works here, is perhaps the ultimate keepsake. Like other projects in this section, it's the kind of gift that goes on giving long after the occasion it was designed to celebrate is over. For instructions and tips for making your own commemorative quilt, please turn the page.

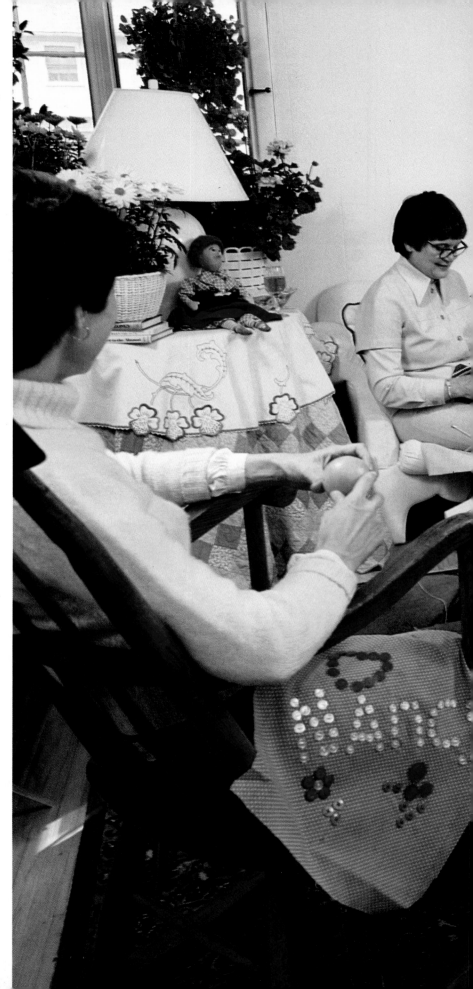

Create a Commemorative Quilt

The friendship quilt is a treasured American tradition, with roots traceable to the pioneer days. Quilts in those days were stitched to commemorate special occasions such as births, weddings, and a neighbor's departure to set up housekeeping in a new town or homestead in a new state.

Why not revive this tradition among your own friends and family? Or craft a quilt with the aid of a community, church circle, school group, or scout troop. Suggestions for designing your own commemorative quilt follow.

Friendship Quilt

The contemporary quilt pictured here and in progress on the preceding pages features 30 different 12x12-inch squares. Unlike quilts created by our pioneer forebears, which were usually either pieced or appliquéd and stitched entirely of cotton or wool, these squares are worked in a variety of craft techniques and materials. Some are suitable for novice crafters; others involve two or more techniques that challenge even the most advanced stitcher.

Squares include crocheted medallions tacked to a fabric background, cross-stitch, needlepoint, appliqué, simple batik, crayon prints, patchwork, cyanotype printing, and acrylic paints on fabric. Even a technique as simple as stitching shirt buttons in a name or design yields an easy to make, but still very personal, square.

The point, of course, is that almost anyone—not just the award-winning stitchers and the master crafters—can make a successful and original contribution to a friendship quilt.

Other equally suitable craft techniques include crewel, smocking, reverse appliqué, pulled or drawn thread work, block printing, and trapunto. Although these squares are worked in different techniques and color schemes, they form a wonderfully lively and congenial whole when you assemble them with sashes and border strips in a strong complementary color or a small print.

Planning the quilt. It's a good idea to get together with all the contributors ahead of time to set the general guidelines for your project. You will need to decide if you want the quilt to match the recipient's home decor or if the squares are to reflect a particular theme or event.

At this time, too, decide whether you want the quilt to be executed in a single technique (such as appliqué) or a limited color scheme or both. If so, choose an appropriate backing fabric and a few basic colors for the quilt top right away, so that each designer will have a general idea of the range of colors to be used. Also decide on the size and number of squares to be completed for the project.

Suggestions for a themed quilt. Keep in mind the tastes and preferences of the recipient. For example, if he or she has a particular interest or hobby, a quilt based on motifs reflecting that interest will be doubly appreciated. If the quilt is intended to celebrate a special wedding anniversary, squares depicting highlights of the couple's life together would be especially appropriate. And, if the quilt is being prepared by neighbors for a family moving away, squares of familiar neighborhood scenes or events will evoke happy memories of old friends when the family settles in their new home.

Designing a square. Before beginning your square, you need to decide whether you want the design to dictate the technique, or whether you want to use a specific technique and plan the design around it.

For example, if you want to do your square in pieced patchwork, the design should feature straight lines and geometric shapes. If the design contains curved shapes, lots of detail, or lettering, use a technique that will give you the best results. Appliqué works well for curved shapes, embroidery provides fine detail, and cross-stitches or fabric paints are particularly suitable for lettering.

To create a pattern, first draw on a sheet of paper a square the same size as one of the finished quilt squares. Think of this box as an empty frame. If you do all your drawing or sketching on sheets of paper placed over this square frame, you can be sure the finished design will be the right size.

To plan your square, don't hesitate to adapt any of the hundreds of traditional quilt block designs that already exist—your choice of color and fabric will make the design uniquely your own.

However, if you're looking for a more "original" subject for your quilt square, there's a wealth of design motifs at your fingertips. Perhaps you could base your design on the recipient's favorite flower or tree, or do a representation of the family pet. If you're not an "artist," trace an appropriate figure from a magazine or child's coloring book (a good source of simple designs).

You also may wish to incorporate one of the recipient's favorite sayings or slogans in the design. Or you could adapt a treasured child's drawing or a decorative motif from textiles or architectural features in the recipient's home.

Finally, be sure that each contributor includes his or her name or initials within the design of each square. Use an indelible fabric marker or simple outline stitches in a corner of the square. You also may want to include one quilt block

with the recipient's name, the date, and a few words concerning the occasion the quilt commemorates.

Assembling the quilt. When all the squares have been completed, assemble them into the finished quilt. Following are general instructions for assembling a 72x86-inch quilt such as the one shown here. If the size and number of squares for your quilt differ from the measurements given here, adjust the materials requirements and the instructions accordingly.

===========HOW TO===========

Materials
Thirty 12x12-inch quilt squares (or number and size desired)
2½ yards of 44-inch-wide solid-color fabric for sashing and borders
5 yards of 44-inch-wide companion print for backing
80x90-inch sheet of polyester quilt batting

Instructions

Lay out the squares in six rows of five squares each. Strive for a good balance of light and dark shades, texture, and color.

From solid-color fabric, cut 25 strips for the horizontal sashes, each 2½x12½ inches. Using ¼-inch seams, sew sashing strips between squares to form vertical strips. Then cut four 2½x87½-inch-long strips; sew these between the vertical rows of squares. Cut additional 2½-inch-wide border strips; stitch them to the ends and sides of the quilt top.

Next, cut and piece the quilt backing fabric to match the front. Place a quilt batt between the top and the backing. Pin and baste it in place. Trim the batting and backing to the finished size. Turn the raw edge of the quilt top ¾ inch over the backing. Then turn under the raw edge ¼ inch and stitch it to the backing.

Machine- or hand-quilt around each square. If desired, add ribbon or yarn tufting in the corners of each square.

continued

→ Work 17 across
→ Work 16 across   In assorted colors
→ Work 12 across

1 Square = 1 Stitch

Cross-Stitched Friendship Square

One of the most delightful squares in our friendship quilt is a cross-stitched version of a familiar rhyme about friends, shown above. It's a quick and easy project to stitch on #22-count hardanger cloth using multicolored scraps of six-strand embroidery floss.

If you have no quilt in the works at the moment, this charming stitchery is equally at home as a pillow top or a framed sampler. Or work the design in needlepoint using continental stitches and left-over yarns. Leave the background unworked or fill it in with basket-weave stitches. Then finish it as an album cover for a special friend.

================ **HOW TO** ================

Materials
13-inch square of #22-count hardanger cloth
One skein of black embroidery floss, plus scraps of floss in a variety of colors

Instructions
Following the pattern, above, cross-stitch the design over two strands of fabric. Use three strands of floss throughout.

Begin in the center of the design and the center of the fabric and work toward the edges. Repeat the heart border (flopped) above the first line of the verse.

Press the finished stitchery on the wrong side using a damp press cloth between the fabric and the iron. Incorporate the square into the quilt; make it into a pillow top; or stretch it over a layer of quilt batting atop a piece of foam-core board (available at art stores), frame, and hang.

To adapt a verse or saying for stitchery, follow these suggestions: First, plan the lettering and border designs on graph paper. Use needlecrafters' alphabets from books or magazines as a guide for lettering, or create your own upper- and lowercase letters.

Transfer the shapes of the letters to graph paper with 10 squares per inch. (Tape together enough sheets of paper so that you can chart out the entire design). One square on the graph paper should equal one cross-stitch on the fabric.

Use simple border designs (such as the hearts, above) to set off the sentiment expressed in the verse or saying. Borders may be worked above and below the lettering, in a box around it, or simply below it.

Chart the design using colored pencils in the shades you intend to use for the stitching. And let your own sense of color and design guide you in the placement and complexity of the border motifs.

Sign Up Your Friends

Here are two crafty ways to keep track of your company: an embroidered adaptation of the Victorian guest-book tradition and a super-simple autograph pillow for your teenager.

Guest-Book Tablecloth

▬▬HOW TO▬▬

Materials
Purchased linen tablecloth
Embroidery floss in colors of your choice
Washable embroidery marker

Instructions
Invite guests at any special gathering—wedding reception or anniversary party, birthday bash or housewarming—to sign the table-cloth with the washable pen. Try to have the signatures as evenly scattered as possible over the cloth. Embroider each signature with two or three strands of cotton floss in simple outline stitches.

Of course, you don't have to wait for a special occasion to launch this project. Using any solid-color tablecloth or pillow as a background, it's a thoughtful idea at anytime. And it's a great way to use up leftover scraps of floss!

Autograph Pillow

▬▬HOW TO▬▬

Materials
½ yard of polished cotton
Rickrack trim and cording
Polyester fiberfill
Fine-point permanent markers

Instructions
Have each guest sign his or her name or scrawl an appropriate sentiment onto fabric; stitch the finished "document" into a pillow.

Stitch a Picture

Turn your sewing machine into a tool that is as handy and as versatile as an artist's pencil. Use this simple technique to "paint" a picture of the family homestead, a vacation cottage, your daughter's college dorm, or any other special "landmark" in a loved one's life. And you don't have to be an artist to get the picture—just follow the design suggestions below.

══════HOW TO══════

Materials
35 mm slide or sketch of a house
Paper, pencil, and marker
Matching rectangles of ecru homespun fabric and Pellon fleece
Sewing machine and brown thread

Instructions

First sketch the house on a piece of paper the size of the project you have in mind (the projects at left were stitched on 13x17-inch rectangles of fabric). If you are unsure of your skill as a draftsman, simply photograph the house on slide film and project the image onto a wall. Then trace the outlines onto paper. Keep the design simple, and eliminate extraneous detail wherever possible.

When you are pleased with the drawing, turn the paper over and retrace the design on the *reverse* side of the paper with a dark marker. The picture will be stitched from the *wrong* side of the fabric, making a mirror image on the right side of the fabric; thus you need a reverse image from which to stitch.

Sandwich the fleece between the fabric (wrong side up) and the house drawing (reverse image up). Pin all three layers together.

Thread the machine and bobbin with brown sewing thread; set it for a straight, medium-length stitch.

Lower or cover the feed dogs; attach a darning foot or other attachment that will allow free movement.

Note: The stitch length will be controlled by the speed and evenness with which you move the fabric beneath the needle. For more tips on creative machine stitchery, see pages 56-57.

With the drawing faceup, grasp fabrics and paper firmly. Guide them beneath the needle; stitch on sketched lines. The finished embroidery will appear on the bobbin side of the layers; tear paper away when sewing is completed.

Stitch the principal parts of the design first; finish details later with freehand machine work. For example, with the fabric on top (shown above), use narrow zigzag stitches to couch strands of floss along the main lines of the design.

Turn your finished stitchery into an album cover, a tote bag, throw pillow, or simply frame and hang.

Piece a Pattern in Wood

Run-of-the-mill lumber scraps and leftover lath supply the makings for these very special mementos. Use the patterns on these two pages as a point of departure for your own wood scrap whimsies.

Quilt Block Puzzle

Here is a puzzle derived from one version of an old "Sawtooth Star" quilt block, but you could easily devise a similar puzzle pattern from any geometric quilt design. Make one as a unique gift for a favorite quilt enthusiast. And if you protect the puzzle with several coats of clear acrylic, it will serve double duty as a handsome hot plate for a quilt-lover's pot of tea.

▆▆▆▆ HOW TO ▆▆▆▆

Materials
12-inch square of ¼-inch plywood for base of puzzle
Scraps of ½-inch-thick pine lumber for puzzle pieces and strips of ½-inch pine for sides of box
Sandpaper, finishing nails
Red, white, blue, green, and black acrylic paints; brushes
Clear acrylic spray coating or polyurethane

Instructions

Enlarge pattern, right, to size (green corner squares are 2¾ inches on a side). You may find it helpful to use graph paper to draft a full-scale pattern. Cut pieces from ½-inch pine scraps.

Note: The heavy black lines on the pattern represent cutting lines; the lighter black lines merely indicate divisions of color. The shapes of the wooden puzzle pieces do not necessarily follow the actual square and triangle divisions of the quilt pattern.

Sand all edges and paint each wooden piece with acrylics, referring to the photograph, above. For the green corner pieces, paint background color first, let dry, then add white flowers.

On those puzzle pieces that are more than one color, mark the division of colors with a narrow line of black paint. Spray the completed puzzle pieces with clear acrylic or protect them with several coats of polyurethane.

To make the box frame, nail ½-inch-wide strips of pine to the plywood base; miter or butt-join the corners. Sand all edges smooth and protect with clear acrylic spray or polyurethane.

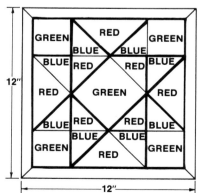

Wood Barn Mosaic

━━━━━━━HOW TO━━━━━━━

Materials
**Scraps of lath, ¼-inch-ply-
  wood, strips of ½-inch pine
Wood glue, paints, brushes**

Instructions
Enlarge the pattern and transfer
it to plywood backing, leaving ½-
inch margin all around for the
frame. Cut strips of lath to size and
glue in place. Accent door, windows, and roof with scraps. Stain
lath with a light wash of acrylic
paints, fabric dyes, or water colors
to allow the grain of the wood to
show through. Frame with ½-inch-
wide pine strips.

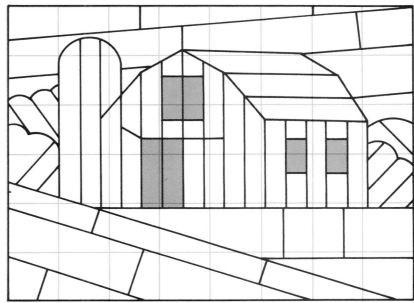

1 Square = 2 Inches

Embroider a Pillow

Some occasions are just perfect for an out-and-out display of sweet sentimentality—and what could make a sweeter or more sentimental gift than this quick-to-stitch cherub pillow?

HOW TO

Materials
½ yard of off-white, medium-weight fabric

3 skeins of gold metallic or colored cotton embroidery floss and needle

Upholstery trim, lace, and scraps of fabric for ruffles

14-inch pillow form or polyester stuffing

Instructions
Enlarge the pattern, right, and transfer it, centered, to a 15-inch square of fabric.

Embroider the pattern in simple outline ·stitches, using either gold threads or three strands of cotton embroidery floss in colors of your choice.

Stitch a double layer· of gathered, 2-inch-wide ruffles (lace and fabric) to the completed pillow front, ½ inch in from edge. Or, add a single ruffle of lace and frame the cherub picture with a row of upholstery trim if preferred.

Back the embroidered pillow front with a matching piece of fabric, stitching it around three sides. Turn, press, stuff, and slip-stitch the fourth side closed.

1 square = 1 inch

Craft a Frame

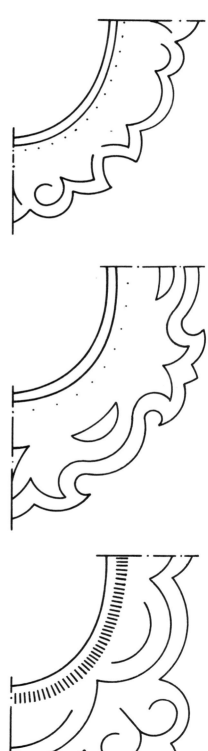

Show off treasured family photos in luxury-look frames cut from foam-core board and "plated" with silver paint.

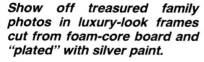

Materials
**Foam-core board, craft knife
Silver spray paint, silver and
    gold paint in jars, brushes
Small metallic beads, glue**

Instructions

Each of the patterns, right, represents ¼ of a full frame. Trace and complete the patterns and cut frames from foam-core board with sharp craft knife. Gently indent along pattern lines with blunt end of a paintbrush. Glue beads in place and paint edges of board to fill in air pockets. Spray the frames with silver paint. Add gold accents with fine paintbrush, if desired.

Design a Collage

Why settle for a drawerful of fuzzy snapshots when you can recapture the spirit of a summer holiday in a one-of-a-kind collage you've made yourself? Use the beach scene above as an inspiration or work from sketches of your own favorite vacation spot. And while you're snipping and pasting, assemble a crafty collage card or two to send to a special friend!

HOW TO

Materials
Mat board and plain note cards
Collection of scrap papers
Spray adhesive, rubber cement, craft knife, scissors

Instructions

Sketch a design on a sheet of paper that is approximately the size of your finished composition. (The seascape, above, is 15x20 inches, and the cards, right, are about 5x7 inches each.) Do not draw any of the shapes directly onto poster board, cards, or colored papers—let the scissors do the design work so the collage will have a spontaneous feeling.

Experiment with different techniques to achieve the effects you want. For example, tear heavy papers, rather than cutting them, for a deckle or wave effect. And use pinking shears for a ridged edge (see violet leaves).

Take advantage of contrasts between mat and shiny papers and textured and smooth surfaces. Weave strips together for a basket or lattice look and incorporate real paper memorabilia (ticket stubs, souvenir napkins, or snapshots) to personalize some compositions.

To assemble the collage, first secure background pieces with spray adhesive. Next, add design details, shuffling smaller pieces around until you are pleased with the arrangement. Tack these in place with spray adhesive or rubber cement. Weight cards and pictures with books and let dry. Finish with a protective coat of clear acrylic spray, if desired.

Personalized Presents

Adding a handcrafted name or a handsome initial is often all it takes to turn a ho-hum item into the perfect gift for someone special. To illustrate our point, we've assembled a charming collection of gifts and embellished each of them with an alphabetically inspired design.

The portfolio of projects here and on the following pages is positive proof that contemporary notions of personalizing go far beyond the engraved lockets and monogrammed sweaters of yesteryear! You'll find suggestions on transferring designs to almost any material, using techniques from woodburning to fabric painting to embroidery. And, we offer patterns for all 26 letters of our illustrated alphabet. Directions for the blocks, box, and bears are on the next page.

Crafter's Alphabet

The perfect project is rarely easy to come by. But happily, good designs—whatever their origin—can frequently be interpreted in several materials or adapted to more than one craft technique. So a clever crafter, like a gourmet cook, soon masters the fine and useful art of inventive substitution!

If you find a design you like, but you do not have the necessary skills or materials to copy it exactly as shown in a book or magazine, don't abandon the project. With a little ingenuity, you can find a way to make that design work for you—by substituting materials, switching the colors, or trying another technique.

To illustrate how a wide variety of craft skills and materials may be utilized, we've parlayed a set of basic alphabet patterns into more than a dozen different projects. The easiest way to adapt a design for crafting is to trace it, then paint it on a surface such as the ceramic dishes, opposite, or the toy box and blocks illustrated on pages 64-65.

Painting on Wood

HOW TO

Materials
Graphite or carbon paper
Woodburning tool
Acrylic or enamel paints
Varnish
Fine brushes

Instructions

To transfer designs to wood, slip graphite paper between the design and the surface; trace outlines with a pencil. Transferred designs may then be woodburned, painted, or both. Woodburning the outlines of a design before painting it gives the pattern added depth and a more rustic look. (If you have never woodburned before, you will want to practice on scrap lumber before tackling the project itself.)

High-quality acrylics or enamels are best for painting on wood. Always check to be sure that the paint and the varnish you intend to use are compatible.

• **Wood Blocks:** Enlarge the letter patterns, pages 75-77, to 8 inches square (including borders), and transfer them to the sides of purchased wooden cubes. Or, make your own blocks using six 10-inch-square pieces of ½-inch pine for each block.

Woodburn and paint the designs, then assemble blocks by mitering the edges and nailing and gluing the blocks together. Protect the finished blocks with several coats of varnish.

• **Toy Box:** Begin with a purchased, unfinished wooden chest. Transfer alphabet motifs to the front of the box to spell "toys" or a child's name, then paint the letters in bright acrylic colors. Varnish the entire box after the paint is dry.

• **Wooden Tray:** To make a tray similar to the one shown on page 68, begin with a purchased 12x17-inch unfinished tray. Transfer a 6-inch-square motif to the center of the tray and add other design elements (such as extra clusters of grapes from the "G"), if desired. Woodburn the design lines, then color portions of the design with paints or permanent markers. Finish with varnish when paint or ink is completely dry.

Painting on Ceramics

HOW TO

Materials
Greenware dishes
Small sponge
Pencil and graphite paper
Glaze pencils
Duncan's E-Z Flow Ultra Clear Glaze

Instructions

Designs transferred to ceramics may be colored and glazed in a number of ways, depending on the materials available in your local ceramics studio and your own preference and skill. Consult your Yellow Pages to find a studio close to you. The studio should be able to provide you with greenware (unfired ceramics), instructions, tools, materials, and special pointers.

When you've assembled materials and selected designs, use a sponge and running water to clean the greenware, wiping it to remove the seams left by the mold. Handle the greenware *very* carefully.

Have the greenware pieces fired to bisque. This will change the grayish greenware to a buff white. (The studio personnel should be able to do this for you for only a nominal fee.)

Use graphite paper to transfer patterns to the bisqueware. The graphite lines on the pieces can easily be erased and will burn out completely during the firing.

Use light and dark glaze pencils to color over the graphite lines and to fill in design shapes. (Blue, black, green, and brown pencils work best. Other colors tend to disappear during the firing.) Apply enough pressure to ensure a solid coating of glaze; sharpen pencils often. Avoid erasing glaze pencils, since the erased marks may reappear as shadows when fired.

Thin the clear overglaze with water to the consistency of light cream. Sponge diluted glaze onto the piece, being careful not to disturb the design. Apply a first coat, dry, then apply a second coat. Have finished pieces fired to glaze.

continued

Painting on Fabric

Painted fabric designs like these can be patched together into any number of projects from clothing to quilts, pillow tops, valances, or place mats—anything to which you wish to add a personal touch.

HOW TO

Materials
Prewashed, preshrunk muslin or other light-colored fabric
Brown or gray fine-point, permanent fabric marker
Acrylics or fabric paints in assorted colors
Narrow (¼-inch-wide), rounded paintbrushes

Instructions
To transfer designs to muslin or other lightweight or light-colored fabrics, slip the motif under a piece of fabric. Allowing adequate margins for seams or hems, trace the design lines with a fine-point permanent marker. Use a light touch and test the marker first on scrap fabric to determine the pressure needed for a thin, sharp line.

To transfer designs to heavier fabric, slide dressmaker's carbon paper between fabric and design. Make closely spaced indentations through the three layers (design, carbon, and fabric) with a needle.

After outlines have been transferred, paint designs in colors of your choice. For a light wash of color, thin acrylic paints with water. (For fabric paints, follow manufacturer's directions.)

To lighten colors, mix a drop of white paint with a few drops of water, then mix this with the color. (Too much white makes colors heavy and opaque.) To mix two colors together, follow the procedure for lightening a shade. Be sure to test colors on scrap fabric before painting the actual design.

Dip brush into color, stroke off excess paint on paper toweling, then paint color carefully and sparingly onto fabric. Paint up to but not over the design lines. Paint is less apt to bleed if a sliver of unpainted fabric is left between colors.

Paint dark colors first, then light colors. Let each area dry thoroughly before painting adjacent areas. When paint is completely dry, heat-set the colors with a warm iron on the wrong side of the fabric.

Note: Colored pencils, crayons, and fabric markers also may be used to decorate fabrics. Use a light touch, and heat-set the applied color on the wrong side of the fabric.

• **Initial patch:** This is an excellent way to experiment with painting a small design. Since you are working with a small square of fabric, there is no risk of ruining an entire garment.

Enlarge the letter pattern of your choice and the border, pages 75-77, to a 6-inch square. Transfer the design to the center of an 8-inch square of prewashed muslin or other light-colored fabric and paint with acrylics or fabric paints as described above. Heat-set the paint by pressing on the wrong side.

Fold under raw edges of the square and appliqué the painted monogram to the bib of a pair of purchased overalls, a jumper, the back of a jacket, or any favorite item of clothing. Or, paint smaller patches (using the patterns just as they are) to make appliqués for pockets, collars, sweaters, and other garments or accessories.

• **Pinafore apron:** Transfer 6-inch square designs for any five letters onto squares of fabric. Paint each motif, using colors of your choice. Heat-set designs as above.

Trim the blocks evenly and sew four of the blocks together to make the skirt of the apron. Hem the sides and lower edges of the skirt and gather across the top. Then hem the sides and top edge of the remaining letter block for the bib. Stitch the gathered edge of the skirt to the lower edge of the bib block. Add grosgrain ribbon ties at the waist and the top of the bib.

Continued

continued

Embroidery is another delightful technique to use for our Crafter's Alphabet. You can easily achieve completely different effects by varying the selection of threads, stitches, and background fabrics.

Monogrammed Robe

━━HOW TO━━

Instructions

Enlarge the appropriate initial, pages 75-77, and transfer it to the left breast or pocket of a purchased robe (or other garment). Slip fabric into a small embroidery hoop to avoid pulling it out of shape as you stitch.

Embroider the initial in satin, stem, and other simple stitches, using cotton, silk, or wool embroidery threads. (For stitch diagrams, see pages 216-217.)

Initial Brooch

━━HOW TO━━

Materials
Scraps of dark cotton velveteen
Small scraps of batting, cardboard, and lining fabric
Silk, cotton, and metallic embroidery threads
Embroidery needle, hoop
Bits of lace, beads, etc.
Pin back, glue

Instructions

Transfer the initial (without enlarging it) to velveteen, simplifying the design if necessary. Embroider the initial and accent portions of the design with beads or bits of lace, if desired. Press embroidery gently on the wrong side.

Cover a 2x2½-inch oval of cardboard with batting; glue in place. Carefully stretch the embroidered initial over the padded form; glue raw edges to the back of the cardboard. Edge with a row of metallic lace, a line of beads, or other trims.

Cut a second piece of fabric slightly larger than the oval. Fold under the raw edges and slip-stitch the fabric to the back of the pin to cover the raw edges. Sew or glue the pin back into place.

Mom and Dad Stitcheries

=====HOW TO=====

Instructions

Enlarge the appropriate letters; transfer them to good quality fabric. Work the motifs in silk, cotton, and metallic threads in colors of your choice. Use satin and outline stitches, couching, French knots, and other simple stitches.

Cut a piece of cardboard to size and pad it with a layer of batting. Stretch the stitchery over the backing, and glue into place. Border with ribbon and frame as desired.

Monogrammed Evening Purse

=====HOW TO=====

Materials

Two 12x28-inch pieces of crepe, satin, or other fabric for bag and lining
Matching rectangle of batting or polyester fleece
2 yards of picot-edged taffeta ribbon
Embroidery floss in a variety of colors
Embroidery needle, hoop

Instructions

Enlarge the letter of your choice to an 8-inch square (including the border). Transfer the design to the purse fabric so the base of the monogram is centered 2 inches above one 12-inch-long edge of the fabric. (This will be the lower edge of the front flap of the purse.)

Embroider the design in stitches, colors, and threads of your choice. Couch gold metallic thread 1 inch from the raw edge of the fabric.

When the embroidery is complete, baste quilt batting or fleece to the back. Baste taffeta ribbon on the right side of the fabric along the seam line (½ inch from the raw edge of the front flap). Position the ribbon so just the picot trim will show. Fold fabric into thirds; sew into an envelope bag. Construct lining and slip-stitch into place.

continued

Imagination and bits of ribbon, beads, lace, and quilled paper swirls are all you need to adorn even the simplest motif. Then craft your design into an elegant box or a sweet, picture-perfect valentine.

Monogrammed Box

====**HOW TO**====

Materials
½ yard each of linen, muslin, and polyester fleece
Pink and blue floss
Beads, buttons, sequins, etc.
Cardboard for box
1-inch-wide satin ribbon in the following colors: 2 yards of pale pink; 2½ yards of pale blue; 1½ yards each of ecru and bluish-purple; ½ yard of medium pink
1½ yards of ¾-inch-wide pale pink satin ribbon
1½ yards each of ½-inch-wide blue and raspberry satin ribbon
1½ yards of ¼-inch-wide ecru satin ribbon
Thread, needle, craft glue

Instructions
The finished size of the box, opposite, is 10½ inches square.

Enlarge the design of your choice to a 6-inch square; transfer it to an 8-inch square of muslin. Embroider the design, then embellish with beads, sequins, or appliqués, if desired. Baste fleece to the back of the square and set aside.

To prepare ribbon points for the box top, cut 1-inch-wide ribbon as follows: 12 pieces of bluish-purple and 4 pieces of pale pink, each 4 inches long; 12 pieces of pale blue and 4 pieces of medium pink, each 4 inches long; and 24 pieces each of pale pink and ecru, each 2 inches long.

Working at the ironing board, press ribbon lengths into pointed shapes (see the photograph). Slip pink 2-inch points inside ecru 2-inch points to make 24 double points. Set ribbons aside.

To make box lid, trim the embroidery to a 6½-inch square, then center and stitch monogram atop an 11½-inch square of linen.

Using the photograph as a guide, arrange ribbon points in three rows around the monogram. Sew the longest points 1 inch from the raw edge of the center square, medium points ½ inch closer, and shortest points butting up against the square. Sew ¼-inch-wide ecru ribbon around the square; knot at the center front.

To finish the lid, pin an 11½-inch square of muslin to the right side of the decorated square. Sew around three sides (½-inch seams), leaving the back edge open. Turn and press. Slip a 10½-inch-square piece of cardboard inside, turn under raw edges of fabric, and whipstitch closed.

Next, referring to the photo, sew bands of ribbon to a 5½x43-inch linen strip. With right sides facing, sew a muslin lining strip to the ribboned strip along one long edge (½-inch seam). Turn; press. Stitch vertical seams in the center of the strip and 10½ inches on either side of center seam. (Ends of strip and lower edge are still open.)

Insert 10½x4½-inch pieces of cardboard between seams and at ends of strip. Turn raw edges to the inside and whipstitch closed. Shape the strip into a square and whipstitch free ends together.

For the bottom, sew 11½-inch squares of muslin and linen together on three sides (using ½-inch seams). Turn, press, insert a square of cardboard, and stitch closed. Sew bottom to sides; sew lid to one side of box top.

Quillwork Initial

====**HOW TO**====

Materials
Mat board
Strips of quilling paper
White paper for letter
Paper doilies
Glue, toothpicks
Scrap of lace trim; frame

Instructions
First, enlarge the initial to desired size and trace it onto a scrap of paper. Reduce the design to its simplest outlines, then transfer these guidelines to the mat board using graphite paper.

Next, cut the basic letter shape from stiff paper and score it gently to give the letter a sculptured look. Glue into place.

Referring to the original letter design for inspiration, embellish the basic letter shape with swirls of quilling. Roll narrow strips of paper tightly around a toothpick to make basic scrolled shapes (refer to a quilling how-to book for tips on creating more elaborate quilled forms). Glue the quilled shapes in place, and also glue on bits of paper lace doilies to add visual interest to the design.

Mat the initial with a ruffle of lace trim; frame as desired.

continued

TIPS & TECHNIQUES

Enlarging and Transferring Designs

The successful completion of a craft project often depends on accurately enlarging, reducing, and transferring a pattern.

Changing the size of any pattern to suit the requirements of a given project is a simple matter when you use one of the several methods described below. When you've mastered these techniques, you'll be able to work from scaled-down designs in craft books and magazines or to adapt designs from other sources—scaling them up or down to suit your needs.

Once the design is the size you need, there are several ways you can transfer the outlines of the pattern to the material on which you wish to work.

Enlarging or Reducing Patterns

Patterns with grids

Most of the patterns in this book appear on grids—small squares (usually printed in blue) laid over the design (usually printed in black). Enlarge or reduce these patterns by drawing a grid of your own on tissue or brown kraft paper, using the scale indicated on the pattern as a guide.

For example, if the scale is "1 square = 1 inch," draw a series of 1-inch squares on the pattern paper and use this grid to enlarge the drawing to the recommended size.

To avoid drawing a grid, purchase sheets of graph paper at an art or office supply store. Graph paper is available in sizes ranging from 1 square to 14 squares per inch. Large sheets are sold by the yard in some art shops or through engineering supply houses. Also, some fabric shops carry pattern-

enlarging tissue with small dots printed at 1-inch intervals. These dots can be connected by pencil lines to form the necessary grids for enlarging or reducing.

To form a working grid for pattern enlargement, count the number of horizontal and vertical rows of squares on the original pattern. With a ruler, mark off the exact same number of horizontal rows of larger squares on your grid paper.

Next, number the horizontal and vertical rows of squares in the margins of the original pattern. Transfer the numbers to corresponding rows on your pattern sheet.

To enlarge the pattern, locate a square on your grid that corresponds with a square on the original. Mark your pattern grid with a dot wherever a design line intersects a line on the original grid.

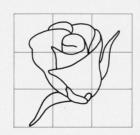

The original design

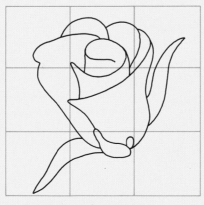

The enlarged design

For best results, visually divide every line into fourths to gauge whether the design line cuts the grid line at the halfway point or somewhere in between.

To sketch in the new, enlarged design on your grid, connect the dots. Mark lightly using a soft pencil until the new, enlarged pattern duplicates the original to your satisfaction. (See the drawings, below left.)

To alter the size of any project with a grid pattern, just make adjustments in the scale of the grid when it is enlarged or reduced. For example, if the instructions call for enlarging the pattern on a grid of 1-inch squares and you want the finished project to be 25 percent larger than called for in the original instructions, simply draw a grid of 1¼-inch squares to work from.

To reduce a design, make a pattern grid with squares that are proportionately smaller than the squares on the original grid. Then proceed to sketch in your new, smaller pattern on the scaled-down grid.

Patterns without grids

Even if the pattern or design for your craft project has no grid, it can be enlarged or reduced if you know either the height or the width of the final pattern size. First, draw a square around the original design. Then draw a diagonal line from the lower left to the upper right corner of the box.

On a sheet of pattern paper, draw a right angle with your ruler. Then extend the bottom line to the exact length of the new pattern.

For example, if you want to enlarge a 3-inch-square design to fit on an 11-inch-wide pillow front, first draw a right angle on the pattern paper and extend the bottom line out to 11 inches.

Next, lay the original design in the corner of the right angle you have sketched on your pattern paper. Matching corners and using a ruler, extend the diagonal on the new pattern sheet. Then draw a perpendicular line up from the end

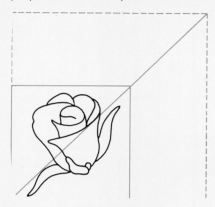

Enlarging without a grid

of the new bottom line to intersect the diagonal, as shown above.

Next, on both the original drawing and the new pattern, draw a second diagonal from lower right to the upper left-hand corner. Finally, divide both the original and the new pattern space in half vertically and horizontally. You will have eight triangular sections from which to work. Transfer the enlarged (or reduced) design as described in the grid pattern method above. (*Note:* If you wish, make additional horizontal and vertical divisions on the pattern and on the new pattern sheet to facilitate the enlargement process.)

Photographic enlargements

There are three methods of enlarging patterns that require no tedious grid work at all; however, they do require special equipment or a modest outlay of cash.

One way is to take a picture of the pattern, using high-contrast black and white slide film. Project the developed slide onto a piece of paper taped to a wall and adjust the image to the size indicated in the instructions for your project (or to the size of your choice). Then trace the pattern onto the paper.

Another way is to check with local libraries and schools for an opaque projector you can borrow or rent. With an opaque projector,

you simply slip the scaled-down pattern into the projector, and it transfers the image to the wall. Again, you will have to trace the projected pattern onto paper.

The third method is to go to a photographic reproduction shop and have the pattern enlarged photographically (often while you wait). Ask for a "positive copy" of the design, specifying the dimensions you want. You can expect to pay from five to ten dollars for each print, depending on the percentage of enlargement.

Transferring Designs

There are several different methods of transferring a pattern from paper onto craft materials. Some methods are applicable for a variety of materials, while others are suitable for one specific surface.

Dressmaker's carbon paper

Dressmaker's carbon (not typing carbon) comes in a range of colors from yellow to black. Select a color that is as close as possible to the color of the fabric you intend to mark, yet still visible. Place the carbon between pattern and fabric, and trace over the design using a tracing wheel or an empty ballpoint pen. Use just enough pressure to transfer the design to the fabric, without tearing the pattern.

Hot transfer pencil

Transfer pencils are especially useful for transferring designs to fabrics that are too opaque to trace through and for transferring complex designs (such as embroidery motifs) to linens, cottons, and other smooth-surfaced fabrics.

Keep the transfer pencil sharp so that lines do not blur. Lightly trace the outlines of the design onto the *back* of the pattern. Then position the pattern, transfer side down, on the fabric and iron the design into place, being careful not to scorch the fabric.

It's a good idea to test your transfer pencil on scrap fabric before you begin because color deposited on fabric does not always

fade when the article is washed or dry-cleaned. Practice drawing on paper, varying the pressure and the sharpness of the point. Also practice ironing the transfer onto fabric until you can mark a line that is dark enough to see while you are working on the project, but faint enough not to show when the project is completed.

"Disappearing" pen

This is a light blue felt-tip marker especially designed for needlework and fabric crafts. Draw or trace the design directly onto light-colored fabrics. Work the design, and when you are finished, simply dampen the fabric and the blue line will disappear. The pen is ideal for tracing designs on sheer fabrics, or for sketching designs freehand.

Basting

This is an efficient way to transfer design lines to dark, soft, highly textured, stretchy, or sheer fabrics. Use this technique to transfer designs to fabrics when other methods described above won't work.

First draw the pattern onto tracing paper and pin it to the fabric. Hand- or machine-baste around the design lines, then tear away the tissue paper and proceed with your project. Remove basting stitches when you've finished with the project (if not covered by appliqué, embroidery, and so on).

Graphite paper

An alternative to carbon paper, graphite paper is ideal for transferring designs to paper, greenware, wood, and other medium- to hard-surfaced materials. It makes a light line that can easily be erased if necessary.

Embossing

Another method of transferring patterns to hard surfaces such as wood, leather, and greenware ceramics is to lightly incise the design on the surface with an empty ballpoint pen or other medium-sharp implement. In good light, the design is visible to the crafter as the pattern is worked, but there are no unsightly ink or graphite lines to be concealed or erased when the project is finished.

Projects with a Personal Stamp

Designer logos are popping up on everything from bibs to britches these days, but you don't have to be a "big name" to produce your own signature crafts. All you need are some rubber name stamps, colored inks, and a little elbow grease!

Check with local office supply stores to see if they take orders for name stamps, or look under "rubber stamps" in the Yellow Pages. Then, with stamps in hand and ink pad at your side, you can print your own designer collection in a twinkling—or create "name brand" gifts for friends, complete with personalized wrapping paper.

HOW TO

Materials
Purchased name stamps
Foam or felt stamp pads
Stamp pad inks
Fabric paints or acrylics
Solid-color wrapping paper and card stock
Muslin or other light-colored fabric

Instructions

To print on paper, you can work with stamp pad inks, acrylics, or latex paint. But use *only* acrylics or fabric paints if you want to make permanent prints on fabric.

Protect work space with newspapers, then saturate stamp pads with ink or thinned paints. Practice printing on scrap paper or fabric first, to determine the amount and consistency of ink to use and how much pressure to apply for a clean print. Printing in horizontal, vertical, or diagonal rows creates a strong, rhythmic pattern. You can achieve more intricate designs by varying the direction, spacing, or color of the stampings.

For fabric projects, stamp the fabric first, and set paint by pressing fabric on the wrong side. Then cut out and complete the project. Use a purchased pattern for the tie. Stamp a 25-inch hemmed square of muslin for the scarf.

Continued

continued

Once you start stamping, you'll find a whole pack of projects taking shape. You might want to print up a gang of these funny, friendly little namesake dolls, or a pile of personalized place mats for each and every member of the family.

HOW TO

Materials
Name stamps
Fabric paints and stamp pads
Muslin fabric and stuffing for
  dolls
Prequilted fabric, bias binding,
  and grosgrain ribbon for
  place mats

Instructions
• **Dolls:** Use the patterns, right, just as they are for small dolls, or enlarge them, if desired.

On muslin, trace a front and back for each doll, adding ½-inch seam allowances all around. Stamp names across the pattern pieces, running the stamped pattern beyond the seam lines. Press printed fabric to set the paint, then cut out shapes.

With right sides together, pin doll backs to fronts. Stitch, leaving an opening; turn the dolls right side out and press. Stuff lightly with fiberfill, and whipstitch the openings closed. Add ribbon trim, if desired.

• **Place mats:** Cut a 12x18-inch oval of prequilted fabric for each mat. Stamp names in diagonal rows across the fabric, allowing space for strips of ribbon between the rows. Press fabric to set the paint. Topstitch ribbon between the rows of stamped names, then bind each mat with bias tape.

Mats and other fabric projects should be washed on a gentle cycle in lukewarm water.

continued

A set of individual alphabet stamps opens up endless possibilities for personal expression, both silly and serious! Stamp out your message of the moment on all types of paper and fabric paraphernalia—from highly personalized note cards to spur-of-the-moment T-shirts designed to commemorate any occasion.

Check art and office supply shops, toy stores, and hobby centers for alphabets in a variety of sizes and typefaces.

Muslin Wall-All

For the ever-present odds and ends in everyone's life, the handy sorter, right, offers a practical solution. Stitch it from inexpensive muslin (or any other light-colored, solid fabric scraps you have on hand), adding as many pockets as you like. Then stamp identifying categories on each of the pockets to match your own private filing system.

HOW TO

Materials
2½ yards of unbleached muslin
½ yard of polyester fleece or quilt batting
Rubber stamps
Inked stamp pad or uninked pads and fabric inks

Instructions

Preshrink the muslin and press. Cut two 13½x20½-inch rectangles from muslin and a matching piece from batting. Layer these three pieces (batting in the middle) and baste them together for backing the wall-all.

From remaining muslin, cut eight 13½x13-inch rectangles for the pockets. Fold each rectangle in half so that the pockets are 13½ inches wide and 6½ inches deep.

Next, practice stamping on scraps of muslin. Use a variety of ink colors and strive for a loose, casual placement of letters. Once you've mastered the lettering, stamp labels on the front of each pocket. Center labels about ½ inch below the folded (top) edge of each pocket strip.

Position the first printed pocket 2 inches down from the top of the

backing. Pin and stitch it in place along sides and bottom (⅝-inch seam allowance). Repeat for the remaining pockets, spacing each one 1¾ inches below the folded top of the preceding pocket.

Trim the edges, round corners slightly, and bind the raw edges with 3-inch-wide bias-cut strips of muslin. Fold in the raw edges of the strip as for purchased bias binding and sew in place. Add narrow muslin loops to the top corners of the wall-all for hanging.

Stamped Samplers

Whether you favor down-home sentiment or a slightly sassier outlook, turn your favorite saying into a no-sew sampler. To mimic embroidered details, cut simple designs (leaves and vines, crowns or flowers) from adhesive-backed foam. Secure the foam to scraps of wood to make your own custom-designed stamps.

═══ HOW TO ═══

Materials
Preshrunk muslin
Alphabet stamps in assorted sizes and typefaces
Dr. Scholl's Adhesive Foam (available in drugstores)
Scraps of wood, scissors
Inked stamp pads or uninked pads and fabric inks
Cardboard and print fabrics for frames
Newspapers, masking tape

Instructions

Press muslin and spread it out on newspapers. Stamp out your message, centering each line as much as possible. Then add embellishments with stamps made from foam and wood scraps. Or, use repeats of a single letter symbol to make a border (such as the Xs around the "WELCOME" sign).

Cut out a cardboard mat, cover with fabric, and tape the muslin into the frame for an instant "sampler."

HOW TO TURN

Rags into Riches

A touch of wit, a snip, and a stitch can turn worn-out clothing into striking, original additions to your wardrobe. From piece-and-patch repairs to start-from-scratch creations, we'll show you how to recycle those ''rags'' into things of beauty for the whole family.

For the simplest salvage operations, you might spruce up a tired blouse or sweater with a new collar and cuffs. Or conceal small stains and worn spots beneath a few artfully placed appliqués or a touch of embroidery.

For more radical reclamations, try something like the strip-quilted jacket and tote shown here. Just snip strips of usable fabric from worn-out clothing, then repiece the strips into better-than-new, one-of-a-kind fabric creations!

For complete instructions, please turn the page.

Super Stripes from Remnants

With fabric scraps culled from other sewing projects, you can create your own striped fabrics for clothing and accessories. Simply machine-piece narrow strips of patterned remnants until you form sufficient yardage for your project.

Quilted Jacket or Tote Bag

Both the strip-quilted jacket and tote bag pictured on the preceding pages are a snap to make using purchased patterns and our simple strip-quilting techniques.

HOW TO

Materials
Purchased pattern
Muslin yardage and quilt batting equal to pattern yardage requirements
Strips of printed cotton fabrics 1½-2½ inches wide

Instructions

Whether you are making a quilted jacket, tote bag, or other item, select a pattern that has a simple shape, a limited number of pattern pieces, and no gathers, tucks, or darts.

Cut all pattern pieces from both muslin and batting. Baste each batting piece to the front of each muslin piece. Next, appliqué individual strips of fabric across the front of each pattern piece, as described in the tips on strip-pieced quilting on pages 90-91.

Trim excess fabric and construct the jacket or bag following pattern instructions. Line, if desired.

To avoid excess bulk, eliminate facings, trim seam allowance at neck and along fronts of jacket, and bind raw edges with bias strips in a complementary fabric.

Child's Backpack

These chevron pattern knapsacks are just right for toting a grade-schooler's homework and snacks.

HOW TO

Materials
1¼ yards of blue Kettlecloth
1½ yards of medium-weight print fabric scraps
19x45 inches of medium-weight batting
Four 1½-inch D rings
Two 1½x2-inch sets of nylon hook-and-loop fastening tape

Instructions

Preshrink all fabric, then cut the patterned fabric scraps into 1¾-inch-wide strips.

Next, cut the blue Kettlecloth as follows: one 13x42-inch rectangle for the lining; two 4x25-inch pieces for the straps; two 8x12½-inch pieces for the side panels; and two 4x5-inch pieces for the ring tabs.

Cut and piece the remaining blue fabric into 1½-inch-wide bias binding.

Cut the batting into matching pieces. Pin and baste batting to wrong side of blue lining piece. With the felt marker, lightly draw a line lengthwise down the center of the panel on the batting side as a guide for centering fabric strips.

With batting side up, machine-sew strips in a chevron pattern from one end of the lining piece to the other as follows: Place a fabric strip wrong side up atop batting at a 45-degree angle so that the strip is centered on the center line (allowing for a ¼-inch seam). Stitch through all layers, then fold and press strip down so that right side shows. Next, place a strip on the opposite side of the center line and repeat the process. When completed, strips should butt against each other as shown in the diagram (see steps 1-4, right).

Trim panel to 11x40 inches and round off bottom corners; baste around edges. Narrowly hem the top (straight) side of the panel.

Turn work over and position the "hook" halves of the fastening tape on the blue side of the panel, 1½ inches up from the curved flap end of the panel. Sew into place. Then position the other half of the fastening tape so that the bottom edges are 10 inches down from the hemmed top of the main panel (see diagram, far right).

For tab rings, fold and stitch each 4x5-inch piece of blue fabric lengthwise to form a 1½x5-inch strip. Slip two D rings onto each strap; fold raw edges under. Sew the rings to the front of the panel so that the edges of the straps are 14½ inches below the top edge.

Next, piece the 4x25-inch strap sections together on the diagonal. Press the seam open, then turn under ¼ inch on all raw edges; press. Place a strip of batting on wrong side of strap, fold strap in half lengthwise; pin, baste, and topstitch strap close to all edges. Fold strap in half along the diagonal seam to form a V; sew strap in place as shown. (Ends of the strap go through D rings.)

Fold each blue side panel in half lengthwise, right sides together, and sew across the narrow edges. Turn, slip a rectangle of batting inside, and baste the remaining two sides closed.

With wrong sides together, sew side panels to main section of backpack using ⅜-inch seams. Make a continuous seam, keeping the needle in the fabric while turning corners. Finally, bind all raw edges with pieced blue binding.

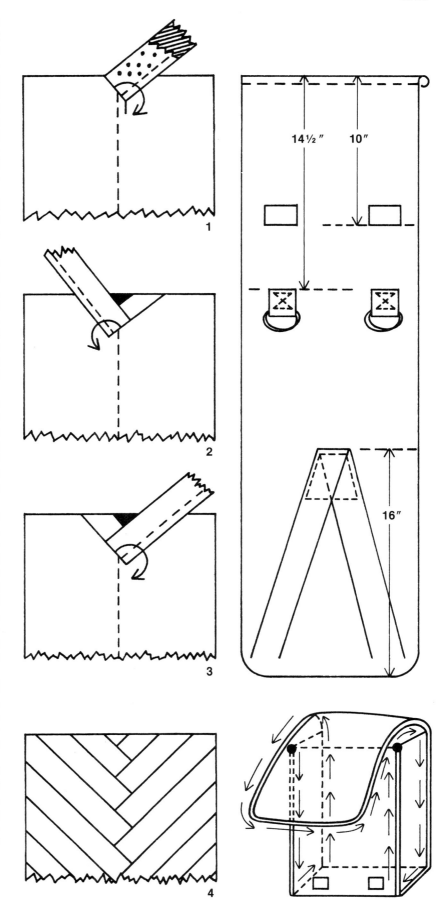

TIPS & TECHNIQUES

Strip Quilting

If you're eager to explore creative yet practical new ways of using remnants, why not try your hand at strip piecing? In terms of economy and invention, it's the ultimate expression of the art of patchwork. You'll be able to use the smallest slivers of the largest assortment of fabrics. And you can combine anonymous—or even discordant—scraps into random patterns of great complexity and beauty.

Collecting Fabrics

Variety is the real spice of strip quilting—a delicious variety of colors, textures, patterns, and piecing possibilities. For example, you might use slivers of 15 or 20 different fabrics to piece a small project —or select and combine 100 or more fabrics for larger projects such as a quilt or a full-length coat.

Naturally, it would be both impractical and expensive to set about assembling three or four different but complementary groups of fabrics on the morning you decide to tackle a simple strip-quilted design, like the jacket on page 87. The secret is to be always on the lookout for appropriate, appealing, or inspirational fabrics for future strip-quilted projects. Start now to stockpile your resources so that when the time comes to begin a project, you have only to pick and choose among your accumulated fabrics for the necessary materials.

Begin by setting aside every long, narrow scrap of fabric that crosses your sewing table. Save strips of cottons, wools, and other "basic" fabrics. But remember that strip-quilted designs can make effective use of remnants of even the most unconventional fabrics!

For example, narrow bands of fabric clipped from hems on slacks and skirts—whatever the fabric—

are ideal for strip piecing. So are sections salvaged from outgrown and outmoded clothing. In fact, clothing is an excellent source of fabrics that are not traditionally suitable for patchwork, but that can add zest to strip designs. Consider using chiffons and sheers, velvets, double-knits, denims, lining fabrics, corduroys, even suedecloth and lightweight leathers.

Such an eclectic selection of materials is part of the fun and excitement of this technique. But, in the interest of practicality, you may want to restrict the kinds of fabrics used in some projects. For example, place mats, baby quilts, and children's backpacks all require frequent washing and therefore should be pieced entirely from easy-care cottons and blends. And for warmth and durability, consider limiting the fabrics in strip-quilted winter wear to wools, wool blends, and similar-weight fabrics.

But for fanciful projects, such as evening clothes, purses, pillows, and special quilts, feel free to mix fabrics with artful abandon! The more shades, textures, patterns, and finishes you combine, the richer your project will look.

Preparing and Storing Fabrics

All clothing should be cleaned, preshrunk, or washed and ironed *before* you cut it into strips. (Narrow strips are likely to tangle and ravel, even if washed by hand.)

Cut away any buttons, zippers, and stained or worn spots from clothes. Then carefully cut the fabric into strips that are 1 to 2 inches wide and as long as possible. For some projects—the yoke of a baby dress, for example—you may wish to experiment with narrower strips, while for others, such as a full-size

quilt, you might include strips up to 3 or 4 inches wide. But 1- to 2-inch-wide strips are appropriate for most projects you undertake.

Press strips flat and roll them into balls. If strips are not long enough to roll up, safety-pin the strips together at one end and loosely fold the strips for storage.

As your stockpile grows, sort strips according to color and store them. Set aside a separate storage container for specialty trims. Used judiciously, these assorted trims can add sophistication and spunk to your strip-quilted projects.

Selecting a Pattern

Although almost any pattern designed to be worked in fabric can be strip-pieced in whole or in part, some patterns are more suitable for this technique than others. Designs with simple lines, a minimum number of pattern pieces, and no tucks or darts will show off strip piecing to best advantage.

In considering a pattern, decide whether you want to strip quilt the entire garment, or confine the piecing to portions of the design, such as the yoke and cuffs of a western-style shirt or the bound border and patch pockets of a vest.

Whether you decide to piece the entire garment or just selected portions, you will use one of two approaches. The first is to piece new yardage from strips of fabric, and then to lay the pattern pieces out on this fabric, cut them out, and stitch them together as though you were working with whole cloth.

The second approach is to cut each pattern piece from lightweight fabric (muslin or organdy), sturdy tissue, or typing paper. The fabric or paper patterns are then used as foundations on which to construct intricate, pieced collages of fabric strips. Then strips are trimmed to match the dimensions of the original pattern piece, and the separate strip-quilted pieces are assembled into the garment.

The method you choose depends largely on the size of the project you plan to make and the intricacy of the piecing.

Selecting a Color Scheme

The projects shown on pages 86-89 all are stitched from random strips of prints and solids in a rainbow of colors. The jacket and tote are patched in muted and pastel shades, and the backpacks are pieced in cheerful primary colors. Monochromatic color schemes are also especially effective in strip piecing; you might choose to work entirely in shades of blue, for example, or to restrict fabrics to one color and a range of neutrals.

As you determine your own color scheme for a given project, spread out fabric strips to get a feel for how they will look together; eliminate any colors that clash too stridently with the "mood" you're trying to establish. But keep in mind that one of the advantages of strip piecing is that the sheer number and variety of colors and materials used in a project often make seemingly discordant colors blend into a pleasingly harmonious whole—much as they do in nature.

Cutting and Piecing Techniques

Once you've chosen a pattern, decided how much of it you're going to piece, and settled on a color scheme, you're ready to begin.

Assemble the fabrics you intend to use, grouping them by color and pattern. If you haven't already done so, cut each strip to an even width from end to end. (The uniform width allows you to maneuver the position and shape of each strip by angling and folding it as you work, rather than having the position of a strip within the design be dictated by its odd shape.)

Cut a foundation for each pattern piece from paper, lightweight fabric, or backing fabric topped with a layer of batting. Be sure to include seam allowances. Piece strips directly onto this foundation.

If you use a paper foundation, pull it away when you have completed piecing and pressing. This is an excellent foundation for appliqués and items that should be light in weight. It also is useful for piecing "yardage": Sew strips of fabric to rolls of shelf paper or even to large rolls of brown kraft paper to create large pieces of "new" fabric, which can subsequently be cut into desired pattern shapes.

Sewing strips to lightweight fabric such as muslin or organdy automatically conceals all seams and provides an instant lining. It also stabilizes pattern pieces when you are mixing fabrics of differing textures and weights.

Piecing against a foundation of batting-topped backing fabric also conceals raw edges, adds stability, and gives the piece a padded, quilted dimension—all in one step! This method is recommended for place mats, jackets, bags, vests, and outerwear. Vary the weight of the batting to suit the project.

Decide on placement of strips —horizontally, vertically, or diagonally across pattern pieces.

To begin stitching, lay the first strip of fabric right side up across one end of the foundation (edges of the strip should extend slightly beyond all seam allowances). Pin and baste the strip into place.

Next, lay a second strip of fabric wrong side up atop the first, with its raw edge even with the raw edge of the preceding strip. Stitch, using ¼-inch seam allowances; press second strip toward body of piece. Continue adding, stitching, and pressing strips until the entire foundation is covered.

Finally, stay-stitch around the edges, trim excess strip fabric to match the outline of the pattern piece, and set aside. Repeat for each portion of the garment that you wish to strip piece.

The method described above yields a surface of narrow, parallel stripes that march in even rows

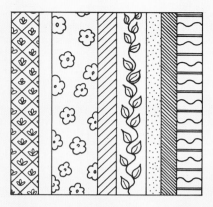

across the pattern piece (see diagram above). Stripes may be all the same width or they may vary from wide to narrow and back again in random fashion.

For a more dynamic and visually interesting surface, make slight changes in the width, angle, and direction of the strips as they are joined (see diagram below).

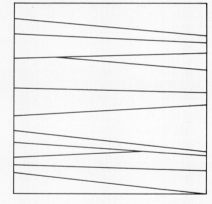

Or, work different portions of the same foundation piece in different directions (see below).

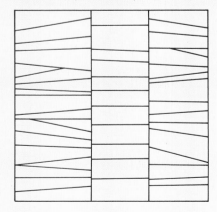

Your own experiments with color and piecing will undoubtedly lead to new and exciting results!

Easy Woolen Patchwork

Here are patchwork projects with genuine Americana flavor and appeal. Like the pieced quilts of yesteryear, this 60-inch shawl and prairie skirt make the best use of fabric bits and pieces. Simply select your favorite scraps, or buy fabric remnants, to create either—or both—of these warm, woolen pieced projects.

Log Cabin Shawl

HOW TO

Materials
1 yard each of 5 different wool challis fabrics in compatible prints, stripes, and paisleys
4 yards of lightweight plaid for backing

Instructions

Lay fabrics in a pleasing sequence to determine the order of the patterns within the design arrangement. Assign a letter (A, B, C, D, E) to each fabric for easy reference when assembling the shawl. Assemble from the center out, using ½-inch seam allowances.

Cut a 21-inch center square (A). Cut remaining A fabric into 5-inch-wide strips. Cut B and C into 4-inch-wide, D into 5-inch-wide, and E into 3-inch-wide strips. Sew together short ends of A strips, piecing them into one long strip. Repeat for remaining strips.

From B, cut two 21-inch lengths and two 29-inch lengths. Stitch the shorter lengths to opposite sides of the center square, then sew the longer lengths to the remaining sides of square (see photograph, above right). Following this procedure, cut and stitch additional lengths to the center in fabrics C, D, A, and E. Press seams open.

For the border, cut all remaining fabric strips into 5-inch lengths. Sew them together at random to make a long 5-inch-wide strip. From this, cut two 61-inch and two 71-inch lengths and sew them to the shawl.

Cut and piece backing fabric to match top. With right sides facing, sew top to back around three sides; turn, press, and topstitch around edges, turning under seam allowances on the opening.

Patchwork Skirt

HOW TO

Materials
Commercial skirt pattern
Wool remnants in assorted plaids, tweeds, and solids

Instructions

Cut remnants into a variety of triangles using pinking shears. On a large flat surface, arrange the shapes, creating the fabric yardage from which to cut the pattern pieces. Don't worry about overlapping the pieces.

Pin the pieces in place. Join by stitching through all of the layers approximately ¼ inch from edges using thread to match fabrics.

Turn fabric to wrong side and clip excess fabric (overlaps). Turn to right side; lay out pattern pieces. Cut out and assemble skirt following pattern instructions.

From solid or plaid fabric, cut and piece ruffle any width desired and twice as long as the circumference of the hem. Hem one edge, gather, and sew to skirt.

continued

Recycle tweed and corduroy into sporty coats-of-many-colors, or stitch small squares of suit-weight flannel into a handsome patchwork scarf.

Man's Jacket

═══HOW TO═══

Materials
Jacket pattern of your choice
Wool and corduroy scraps or remnants equal to yardage requirements
Notions indicated on pattern

Instructions

Pick a jacket pattern with interesting piecing, then carefully select complementary remnants to make up the required yardage.

We started with a wool plaid for the jacket front, and used coordinating navy, gray, and rust corduroys and tweeds for the remaining pattern pieces. Cut pattern pieces from the various fabrics, then follow the pattern instructions to complete the jacket. Line, if desired.

Woman's Jacket

═══HOW TO═══

Materials
Jacket pattern of your choice (with shawl collar as shown)
Wool and corduroy fabric scraps equal to yardage requirement
Satin for shawl collar
Notions indicated on pattern
3-ply crewel yarn
Dressmaker's carbon paper
Embroidery hoop and needle

Instructions

Using dressmaker's carbon paper, transfer outlines of upper collar and front facing patterns onto the front of satin fabric. Do not cut out the pieces.

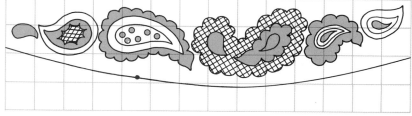

1 Square = 1 Inch

Enlarge the pattern, above, and transfer to satin collar. Position design carefully so motifs fall on front of collar, as shown.

Keeping fabric taut in a hoop, use one ply of yarn for embroidery. Work outline stitches on shaded areas with grids and satin stitches on remaining areas. Cut out the embroidered collar piece.

Cut out the remaining pattern pieces and complete the jacket according to the pattern instructions.

Wool Patch Scarf

═══HOW TO═══

Materials
Scraps of suit-weight wool
Lightweight cotton flannel
Scrap yarn for fringe

Instructions

Using ¼-inch seams, sew eighteen 6-inch wool squares into two rows of nine squares each. Line scarf with flannel; add fringe.

Very Special Vests

These elegantly eclectic vests are one way to display even the smallest fabric treasures to advantage. Small rectangles and squares of tie silk—paisleys, stripes, plaids, and intriguing prints—are pieced together in his vest, above. Hers, opposite, is a delightfully feminine pastiche of lace and ribbons and embroidered bits and pieces.

Whether you use flea market and thrift shop finds or heirloom odds and ends, making each vest requires considerable time and patience. But the one-of-a-kind results are worth every snip and stitch!

Man's Crazy Quilt Vest

HOW TO

Materials
Man's vest pattern of your choice
Satin lining fabric for vest lining and back (see pattern for yardage)
Scraps of medium-weight silk and satin lining fabrics and assorted necktie scraps for pieced vest front
1 yard of muslin
Fusible webbing
Assorted colors of embroidery floss; embroidery needle
Notions as indicated on pattern

Instructions
Cut vest fronts from preshrunk muslin and mark seam allowances on the right side of the fabric. Place muslin fronts faceup on a table to plan the placement of the fabric scraps and tie pieces to best advantage.

Strive for an even balance of patterns and colors on each side of the vest front (refer to the photograph for inspiration). When you are satisfied with the arrangement, pin scraps and ties in place on the muslin, turning under the raw edges. Trim pieces to match the outer edges of the pattern pieces wherever necessary.

Working with one piece of fabric at a time, attach the patches to the muslin backing with fusible webbing. When all the pieces are secure, slip-stitch fabrics in place so all edges are flat.

If desired, use two or three strands of embroidery floss in complementary colors to feather-stitch around each square or triangle (as for a crazy quilt).

Complete the vest according to the pattern instructions, lining front panels to conceal piecing and the underside of the stitches.

Woman's Sampler Vest

======HOW TO======

Materials

Simple, straight-line vest pattern without darts
1¾ yards of muslin
1¾ yards of cotton print fabric for lining
Scraps of lace edgings, ribbons, and doilies
Assorted pieces of print, striped, and plaid fabrics
Notions indicated on pattern

Instructions

Cut all pattern pieces, except facings, from preshrunk muslin. (Because vest will be lined, facings may be discarded.) Mark seam allowances on right side of each muslin piece.

Lay out muslin fronts, right-side-up, and cover each side with a collage of bits and pieces of fabric and lace. Work the design from the shoulders down, making details, colors, etc., on both sides of the vest match or balance.

When you have a pleasing arrangement, pin, baste, and slip-stitch all pieces in place. Turn under raw edges and overlap fabric scraps where necessary. Press appliquéd pieces on wrong side. Repeat procedure for vest back.

Sew front and back pieces together at the shoulder and side seams; press the seams open.

If the vest pattern has pockets (as shown), cut pocket pieces from muslin; appliqué with lace and fabric as for vest. Line each pocket with contrasting print fabric and stitch to front of vest.

Cut and piece lining for vest. Press seams open. With *wrong* sides together, pin lining inside vest. Baste lining to vest around edges and armholes, stitching ½ inch from the raw edges. Trim seam allowances to ¼ inch.

Cut and piece 1½-inch-wide bias strips from contrasting fabric; bind edges and armholes of vest. Slip-stitch binding in place.

We omitted buttons and buttonholes on this design, but they may be added, if desired.

Elegant Accessories

Quick-to-craft collars like these transform a plain-Jane top into something special.

Lace Collar

═══════ HOW TO ═══════

Materials
1⅓ yards of 7-inch-wide lace
1¼ yards of ¾-inch-wide satin ribbon

Instructions
Turn under the raw edges at each end of the lace strip and hem them by hand. Then run a line of small gathering stitches 1½ inches below the top edge of the lace. Gather the strip to 15 inches and tie off.

Center ribbon over the gathering stitches and tack it in place. Tie the collar over anything from blouses to sweatshirts, and secure overlapping edges with decorative ceramic pins.

Button Collar

═══════ HOW TO ═══════

Materials
½ yard of medium-weight, linenlike fabric for collar and lining
¼ yard of muslin
55 white, four-hole shirt buttons for flowers
11 small pearl buttons
1 skein each of #5 pearl cotton in green and blue
1 yard of lace edging
1 yard of narrow satin ribbon

Instructions
Enlarge the pattern, right, and add ½-inch seam allowances all around. Cut two pattern pieces from linen and one from muslin. Sew the muslin interfacing to the wrong side of one linen piece.

Mark seam allowances on the wrong (muslin) side of the collar. Mark each flower center (indicated by dots on the pattern) on the right side of the collar. Sew a pearl but-

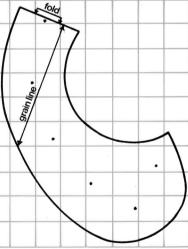

1 Square = 1 Inch

ton in place for each of the 11 flower centers. Sew five shirt buttons around each center with blue pearl cotton; embroider leaves in green lazy daisy stitches.

Baste lace edging in place. Sew lining to collar; trim seams, turn, press, and slip-stitch closed. Add ribbon ties.

Handkerchief Collar

═══HOW TO═══

Materials
Two 12- to 14-inch-square embroidered handkerchiefs
1⅓ yards of satin ribbon

Instructions

With right sides facing and patterns aligned, sew the two squares together diagonally across one plain corner, 2 inches above the point. Trim seam and press open. Fold piece in half diagonally, wrong sides together; press.

Place seam at center back and draw right and left points around neck. Mark position for ties with pins. Cut ribbon into four equal pieces; tack to collar at pin points.

To wear, slip collar around neck; tie ties. Fold neck edge to form a soft roll, allowing collar to lie flat.

Family Sweaters to Knit and Crochet

Crayon colors and unexpected patterns make these quick-knit sweaters a set of real show-stoppers. We used double strands of Coats and Clark Red Heart 4-ply hand-knitting yarn for all three sweaters, but you can substitute any 4-ply knitting worsted of your choice.

Woman's Checkerboard Pullover

Instructions are for sizes 8-10; changes for sizes 12-14 and size 16 follow in parentheses. The bust measurement is 31½ (34-36, 38) inches.

═══HOW TO═══

Materials
24½ (28, 31½) ounces of amethyst yarn (color A)
3½ ounces of off-white yarn (color B)
Knitting needles in sizes 9 and 11 or size to obtain gauge

Gauge: With larger needles over st st, 3 sts = 1 inch; 4 rows = 1 inch.
Knitting abbreviations: See pages 212-213.

Instructions
Note: Use 2 strands of yarn held tog throughout. Back of pullover is worked in one piece. Lower Ribbing is worked after Back is completed. Front of pullover is worked in 4 strips, then strips are sewn together. Lower Ribbing is worked after Front is completed.

Back: Beg at lower edge with 2 strands of A and larger needles, cast on 52 (58, 62) sts. Work in st st until total length measures 13½ (14, 14) in., ending with a p row.

Armhole shaping: Continuing in st st, cast off 3 sts at beg of next 2

rows—46 (52, 56) sts. Work even until total length past beg of armholes measures 6 (6½, 7) in., ending with a p row.

Right neck shaping: K across 14 (16, 17) sts; sl rem sts to holder. Working over the sts on needle only, dec 1 st at neck edge on next row and at same edge every row 3 times in all. Cast off rem 11 (13, 14) sts.

Left neck shaping: Leaving center 18 (20, 22) sts on holder, sl next 14 (16, 17) sts to larger needle. Attach 2 strands A at neck edge and k across. Complete as for other side.

Front: First strip: Beg at lower edge with 2 strands of A held tog and larger needles, cast on 14 (16, 17) sts. Work in st st for 18 (20, 22) rows. Cut 1 strand A, attach B. With 1 strand A and 1 strand B held tog, continue in st st for 18 (20, 22) rows. Fasten off B, attach another strand A. Rep last 36 (40, 44) rows for checkerboard pat. Continuing in checkerboard pat, work until total length measures 13½ (14, 14) in., ending with a p row.

Left armhole shaping: Continuing in checkerboard pat, cast off first 3 sts; complete row. Work even in checkerboard pat until total length past beg of armholes measures 7 (7½, 8) in., ending at armhole edge. Cast off rem sts.

Second strip: Beg at lower edge with 1 strand A and 1 strand B held tog and larger needles, cast on 14 (16, 17) sts. Work in st st for 18 (20, 22) rows. Fasten off B, attach another strand of A and continue in st st for 18 (20, 22) rows. Fasten off 1 strand of A, attach B. Rep last 36 (40, 44) rows for alternate checkerboard pat. Continue in checkerboard pat until total length measures 13½ (14, 14) in., ending with a p row. Mark last row. Continue in checkerboard pat until total length from marked row measures 5 (5½, 6) in., ending with a k row.

Left neck shaping: Row 1: Continuing in checkerboard pat, cast off first 7 (9, 8) sts for neck edge, complete row continuing in pat, dec 1 st at neck edge on next row and every row until 1 st rem. Fasten off.

Third strip: Work same as for First Strip until total length measures 13½ (14, 14) in., ending with a p row. Continue in checkerboard pat until length past marked row measures 5 (5½, 6) in., ending with a p row.

Right neck shaping: Row 1: Continuing in pat, cast off first 7 (9, 8) sts for neck edge; complete row. Complete as for Second Strip.

Fourth strip: Work in checkerboard pat same as for Second Strip until total length is 13½ (14, 14) in., ending with a k row.

Right armhole shaping: Continuing in pat, cast off first 3 sts; complete row. Complete to correspond with First Strip.

Aligning strips in order from right to left, sew strips tog.

Sleeves: Beg at lower edge with 2 strands A held tog and smaller needles, cast on 28 (30, 32) sts. Work in k 1, p 1 ribbing for 2½ in. Change to larger needles and st st, inc 1 st at each end on next row and every 6th row until 42 (46, 48) sts are on needle. Work even until total length measures 17 (17½, 18) in. Mark each end of last row for end of sleeve seam. Continue in st st for 4 rows more. Cast off.

Pin pieces to measurements, dampen, and leave to dry.

Lower back ribbing: With right side facing and 2 strands of A held tog and smaller needles, pick up and k 52 (58, 62) sts across lower edge. Work in k 1, p 1 ribbing for 2½ in. Cast off loosely in ribbing. Work Lower Front Ribbing similarly. Sew left shoulder seam.

Neckband: With right side facing, 2 strands of A held tog, and smaller needles, pick up and k 4

Continued

continued

sts on right back neck edge, k the 18 (20, 22) sts on back holder, pick up and k 4 sts on left back neck edge, pick up 28 (30, 30) sts along entire front neck edge—54 (58, 60) sts. Work in k 1, p 1 ribbing for 1 inch. Cast off in ribbing.

Sew right shoulder seam including neckband; side seams; sleeve seams to markers. Sew in sleeves, sewing side edges of sleeve rem free to cast-off sts of underarm.

Man's Checker-board Pullover

Instructions are for size 38; changes for sizes 40, 42, and 44 follow in parentheses. Chest = 38 (40, 42, 44) inches.

══════ HOW TO ══════

Materials
26 (28, 35, 37) ounces of wood brown yarn (color A)
3½ ounces of off-white yarn (color B)
Knitting needles in sizes 9 and 11, or size to obtain gauge given below

Gauge: With larger needles over st st, 3 sts = 1 inch; 4 rows = 1 inch.

Abbreviations: See page 212.

Instructions
Note: Use 2 strands of yarn held tog throughout. Back is worked in 1 piece. Lower Ribbing is worked after completion of Back. Front is worked in 4 strips, then strips are sewn tog. Lower Ribbing is worked after Front is completed.

Back: Beg at lower edge with 2 strands of A held tog and larger needles, cast on 57 (61, 65, 69) sts. Work in st st until total length is 15½ (15½, 15½, 16) inches; end with a p row.

Armhole shaping: Continue in st st, cast off 4 sts at beg of next 2 rows—49 (53, 57, 61) sts. Work even until length past beg of armholes is 8 (8½, 9, 9½) inches; end with a p row.

Right shoulder and neck shaping: Row 1: Cast off first 6 (6, 6, 7) sts, k until 11 (13, 14, 15) sts are on right-hand needle, k 2 tog, sl rem 30 (32, 35, 37) sts to holder. *Row 2:* P. *Row 3:* Cast off first 6 (6, 6, 7) sts, k to last 2 sts, k 2 tog. *Row 4:* P. Cast off rem sts.

Left neck and shoulder shaping: Leaving center 11 (11, 13, 13) sts on holder, sl next 19 (21, 22, 24) sts to larger needle, attach 2 strands A at neck edge. *Row 1:* K 2 tog; k across. *Row 2:* Cast off first 6 (6, 6, 7) sts; p across. *Rows 3-4:* Rep last 2 rows. Cast off rem sts.

Front: First strip: Beg at lower edge with 2 strands A held tog and larger needles, cast on 15 (16, 18, 18) sts. Work in st st for 20 (22, 22, 24) rows; end with a p row. Cut 1 strand A, attach B. With 1 strand A and 1 strand B held tog, continue in st st for 20 (22, 22, 24) rows. Fasten off B, attach another strand A. Rep last 40 (44, 44, 48) rows for checkerboard pat. Continuing in checkerboard pat, work until total length is 15½ (15½, 15½, 16) inches; end with a p row.

Left armhole shaping: Continuing in checkerboard pat, cast off first 4 sts; complete row. Work even in checkerboard pat until total length past beg of armholes is 8 (8½, 9, 9½) inches; end at armhole edge.

Shoulder shaping: Row 1: Cast off first 6 (6, 7, 7) sts; complete row. *Row 2:* Work across. Cast off rem sts.

Second strip: Beg at lower edge with 1 strand A and 1 strand B and larger needles, cast on 15 (16, 16, 18) sts. Work in st st for 20 (22, 22, 24) rows. Fasten off B, attach A and continue st st for 20 (22, 22, 24) rows. Fasten off 1 strand of A, attach B. Rep last 40 (44, 44, 48)

rows for checkerboard pat. Work in pat until total length is 15½ (15½, 15½, 16) inches; end with a p row. Mark last row. Continue in checkerboard pat until length from marked row is 5 (5½, 6, 6½) inches; end with a k row.

Left neck shaping: Row 1: Work across first 4 (4, 5, 6) sts, sl these sts to a holder for neck edge; complete row. *Row 2:* Work across, dec 1 st at neck edge. *Row 3:* Dec 1 st at neck edge; complete row. Rep last 2 rows once more. Work even over 7 (8, 7, 8) sts until total length past marked row is 8½ (9, 9½, 10) inches; end with a p row. Cast off.

Third strip: Beg at lower edge with 2 strands of A held tog and larger needles, cast on 15 (16, 16, 18) sts. Work checkerboard pat same as for First Strip until length is 15½ (15½, 15½, 16) inches. Mark last row worked. Continue in checkerboard pat until total length past marked row is 5 (5½, 6, 6½) inches; end with a p row.

Right neck shaping: Row 1: Work across first 4 (4, 5, 6) sts, sl these sts to holder for neck edge, complete row. Complete to correspond with Second Strip.

Fourth strip: Beg at lower edge with 1 strand each of A and B held tog and larger needles, cast on 15 (16, 18, 18) sts. Work checkerboard pat same as for Second Strip until total length is 15½ (15½, 15½, 16) inches; end with k row.

Right armhole shaping: Continuing in pat, cast off first 4 sts; complete row. Work to correspond with First Strip. Align strips in order from right to left; sew strips tog.

Sleeves: Beg at lower edge with 2 strands of A held tog and smaller needles, cast on 30 (30, 32, 32) sts. Work in k 1, p 1 ribbing for 11 rows, inc 5 sts evenly spaced on last row—35 (35, 37, 37) sts. Change to larger needles, work in st st for 6 (6, 4, 4) rows. Inc 1 st at each end on next row and every

6th row until 49 (51, 55, 57) sts are on needle. Work even until total length is 17 (18, 18, 19) inches; end with a p row. Mark each end of last row for end of sleeve seam. Continue in st st for 4 rows more. Cast off. Pin pieces to measurements, dampen, and leave to dry.

Lower back ribbing: With right side facing and 2 strands of A held tog and using smaller needles, pick up and k 58 (62, 66, 70) sts. Work in k 1, p 1 ribbing for 9 rows. Cast off in ribbing. Work Lower Front Ribbing similarly. Sew right shoulder seam.

Neckband: With right side facing, 2 strands of A held tog, smaller needles, and beg at left shoulder, pick up and k 16 sts on left front neck edge, k across sts on front stitch holders, pick up and k 21 sts on right front and right back neck edge, k across sts on back holder, pick up and k 6 sts on left back neck edge—62 (62, 66, 68) sts. Work in k 1, p 1 ribbing for 5 rows. Cast off in ribbing.

Sew left shoulder seam including neckband; side seams; sleeve seams to markers. Sew in sleeves, sewing side edges of sleeves rem free to cast-off sts of underarm.

Girl's Log Cabin Pullover

Instructions are for size 5; changes for sizes 7 and 9 are in parentheses. Bust = 30 (31, 32) inches. Refer to diagram, right, as you work.

===HOW TO===

Materials
10½ ounces of skipper blue yarn (color M)
2 ounces each of off-white (color O), amethyst (A), paddy green (B), lavender (C), yellow (D), pale rose (E), vibrant orange (F), clear blue (G), and jockey red (H).
Knitting needles, sizes 9 and 11
9 yarn bobbins

Gauge: With larger needles over st st, 3 sts = 1 inch; 4 rows = 1 inch.

Abbreviations: See page 212.

Instructions
Note: Use 2 strands of yarn held tog throughout. *Back:* Beg at lower edge with 1 strand of M and 1 strand of O held tog and smaller needles, cast on 44 (46, 48) sts. Work in k 1, p 1 ribbing for 2 (2½, 2½) inches. Fasten off O, attach another strand of M. Change to larger needles. With 2 strands of M held tog, work in st st until work is 12½ (12½, 13) inches. Mark each end of last row for top of side seam. Continue in st st until length past markers is 6 (6½, 7) inches, end with a p row.

Shoulder shaping: Cast off first 12 (12, 13) sts for first shoulder, sl next 20 (22, 22) sts to a holder; cast off rem 12 (12, 13) sts.

Note: At this point wind bobbins with 2 strands of colors B, A, F, M, and H; wind rem bobbins with 1 strand of D and O, C and O, E and O, G and O.

Front: Work same as Back until ribbing is complete, inc 1 st at each end on last row of ribbing—46 (48, 50) sts. Fasten off O; attach 1 strand of M. Change to larger needles. (*Note:* Front is worked in 4 strips to neck shaping.)

First strip: Row 1: With 2 strands of M held tog, k across first 2 (3, 4) sts, sl rem 44 (45, 46) sts to a holder to work later. Continue in st st over the 2 (3, 4) sts until work is 12½ (12½, 13) inches; mark outer edge of last row worked for top of side seam. Continue in st st until work equals that of Back, ending with a p row. Cast off.

Second strip: With right side facing and 2 strands of A held tog, k across next 21 sts on holder; leave rem sts on holder. *Row 2:* P. *Row 3:* K. Rep last 2 rows 0 (0, 1) time more. (*Note:* Design is worked in st st with 2 strands of indicated colors held tog throughout. When changing colors, twist colors not in use around the other to prevent making holes. Attach new colors as needed.) Follow every knit row on chart from right to left and every purl row from left to right. Now work design as follows: *Row 1:* With A p 3, with B p 2, with C and O p 14, with D and O p 2. Beg with

Row 2 on chart, follow chart until Row 29 is complete. With A work 3 (3, 5) rows. Now rep Rows 1-29 on chart once more.

Neck shaping: Row 1: Work first 11 (10, 10) sts, sl rem 10 (11, 11) sts to a holder. *Row 2:* P across. Cast off. *Third strip:* Work same as Second Strip to neck shaping. *Neck shaping:* Sl first 10 (11, 11) sts to a holder, with D and O k across the 11 (10, 10) sts. *Row 2:* P across. Cast off. *Fourth strip: Row 1:* With 2 strands of M k across rem 2 (3, 4) sts. Complete as for First Strip. Sew strips tog.

Sleeves: Beg at lower edge with smaller needles and 1 strand of M and 1 strand of O held tog, cast on 22 (24, 26) sts. Work ribbing as for Back for 2 inches. Fasten off O. With 2 strands of M and larger needles, work in st st, inc 1 st at each end on next row and every 8th row until 36 (40, 42) sts are on needle. Work even until work is 16 (17, 17) inches, end with a p row. Cast off.

Pin pieces to measurements, dampen, and leave to dry. Sew left shoulder seam.

Neckband: With 1 strand M and 1 strand O held tog and smaller needles, k across sts on back holder, pick up and k 2 sts along left front neck edge, k across sts on front holder, pick up and k 2 sts along right front neck edge—44 (48, 48) sts. Work in k 1, p 1 ribbing for 3 rows. Cast off in ribbing.

Sew right shoulder seam including neckband. Sew side seam to markers. Sew sleeve seams. Sew in sleeves.

Continued

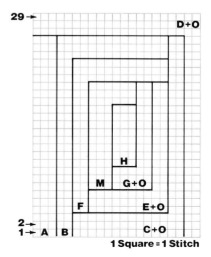

1 Square = 1 Stitch

continued

Girl's Crocheted Sweater

Classic granny squares are the basic building blocks for this cheerful crocheted jacket. And as for colors, anything goes! Use up every available scrap of sport-weight yarn for the floral centers, then frame each square with a round of black to tie the colors together.

Best of all, there are no fancy stitches and no counting and measuring to keep track of. Once you have mastered the granny square pattern and turned out a sweater or two, you may find yourself stitching and stockpiling the squares for future projects.

The simple 2½-inch squares can be pieced and parlayed into dozens of different designs, limited only by your time, imagination, and yarn supply!

The sweater shown is approximately a size 8. To change the size of the sweater for your child, simply add or subtract granny squares to the length or width of the design as you assemble the sweater.

HOW TO

Materials
6 balls (1.75 ounces) of black Unger Roly Sport yarn, or an equivalent amount of any sport-weight yarn, for main color
Approximately the same amount of scraps of sport-weight yarn in various colors for centers of squares
Size F aluminum crochet hook, or size to obtain gauge

Gauge: One square measures 2½x2½ inches.

Abbreviations: See page 214.

Instructions

Granny square—Rnd 1: With any color ch 4; sl st to form ring. Ch 3 (counts as first dc), 2 dc in ring, ch 1, (3 dc in ring, ch 1) 3 times; sl st to top of ch-3. Fasten off.

Rnd 2: With another color, join in any corner sp, ch 3 (counts as first dc), 2 dc in corner sp, ch 1; continue around square, making a 3-dc grp in every sp of previous rnd *and* making a (3 dc, ch 1, 3 dc) grp in every corner sp. Fasten off.

Rnd 3: With black, rep Rnd 2.

Back: Make 42 squares, following instructions above. Arrange the squares in a pleasing pattern, balancing colors, lights, and darks. Arrange the squares in six vertical rows with seven squares in each row. Sew, weave, or crochet the squares together using black yarn.

Front: Make 40 granny squares, following the instructions above. Divide the squares in half: use 20 squares for the left half of the sweater and 20 squares for the right half.

For the left front, align two vertical rows of seven squares each for the side edge. (As you work, strive for a pleasing and sprightly balance of colors and of lights and darks.) Align one vertical row of six squares for the center edge, keeping all three rows flush at the bottom of the piece. Secure pieces together by sewing, weaving, or crocheting with black yarn.

For the right half, align two vertical rows of seven squares each for the side and shoulder edge and one row of six squares for the center edge; stitch, weave, or crochet the squares together. Do not join the center edges.

Sleeves: Make 30 squares for each sleeve. Align squares in six vertical rows of five squares for each sleeve; stitch, weave, or crochet together.

Assembly: With right sides together, secure each front piece to the back by joining the two topmost squares of the front pieces to the corresponding squares of the back. Lay the front/back assembly out flat.

Position the sleeves against the assembly by aligning a six-square row of the sleeve with the center six squares of the front/back pieces. Stitch, weave, or crochet in place. (This joining forms the dropped shoulder.)

Sew together five rows of the sleeve to form a tube; secure the remaining four squares along the front and back pieces to form side seams. Turn up bottom row of sleeve to form cuff.

Collar: With right side facing, attach black at center edge of right front side. (Join yarn in corner sp of top square.) Ch 1, sc in each of next 3 dc, sk sp, sc in each of next 3 dc, sk sp, hdc in first dc of grp, dc in each of next 2 dc in grp, tr in each of next 3 adjacent corner sps, dc in each of next 2 dc, hdc in last dc of grp.

Continue around neck opening, making sc in each dc around and sk sp; round other front corner as before. Change to an accent color; turn. Ch 3 (counts as first dc) and dc in each st around opening. Fasten off.

Make a picot edging as follows: Attach black; ch 1 and sc in 2nd st from hook, * ch 3, sl st in same st as sc, sc in next st. Rep from * around. Fasten off.

Cuffs: With right side facing, join black in any dc; work sc around cuff edge. Drop black, attach a second color and work dc around. Drop color, attach black; work picot edging around as for Collar. Fasten off. Rep for rem sleeve, using a third color.

Right front border: Attach markers in each of the center sts of each of the six squares along front edge. Attach black in bottom corner sp; ch 1, sc in each dc across to marker, sc in same st as marker, ch 7, sc in same st as marker, sc to the next marker. Continue across edge in this manner, making a ch-7 lp in each marked st.

Left front border: Mark center sts of six border squares along left front edge. Attach black at top edge, and make six ch-7 lps at each marker as for Right Front Border.

Bottom: Attach black in bottom corner sp of right front. Work sc in

each dc across; drop black. Join a fourth accent color and work dc in each sc across; drop accent color. Attach black and work a row of picot edging across. Fasten off.

Ties: Make six ties, each in a different color. With two strands, ch 70; fasten off. Thread a tie through corresponding lps on each border; tie with a bow.

Accessories to Knit and Crochet

This colorful mix-and-match assortment of hand-stitched accessories makes marvelous use of every last ounce of worsted yarn in your workbasket.

We used Coats and Clark Red Heart 4-ply hand-knitting yarn for the caps, scarves, and mittens, but you may want to adapt the color combinations and stripe patterns to suit your own supply of scraps.

Crocheted Cap

Instructions include both a small- and large-size ski cap for children.

▬▬▬ HOW TO ▬▬▬

Materials
1 skein (3.5 ounces) each of two colors of Coats and Clark Red Heart 4-ply hand-knitting yarn
Size H (I) aluminum crochet hook, or size to obtain gauge

Gauge: 4 sc = 1 inch; 4 rows = 1 inch.
Abbreviations: See page 214.

Instructions

Note: When rnd is complete, sl st into first st made to join; ch 1 and sc (counts as first sc of rnd) in joining. Crown is worked in 1 color; brim is worked in contrasting color. If desired, work entire cap in 1 color. Work both sizes similarly up through Rnd 17.

Crown: With 1 color, ch 5. Sl st to form ring, ch 1. *Rnd 1:* Work 12 sc in ring. *Rnd 2:* * 2 sc in sc, sc in next sc. Rep from * around—18 sc. *Rnds 3-4:* Work even. *Rnd 5:* Rep Rnd 1—27 sts. *Rnd 6:* * 2 sc in sc, sc in each of next 2 sc. Rep from * around—36 sts. *Rnd 7:* Rep Rnd 6—48 sts. *Rnds 8-10:* Work even. *Rnd 11:* Rep Rnd 5—64 sts. *Rnds 12-13:* Work even. *Rnd 14:* * 2 sc in sc, sc in each of next 8

sc—72 sts. *Rnds 15-17:* Work even. *For larger size only: Rnd 18:* * 2 sc in sc, sc in each of next 9 sc—80 sts. *Both sizes:* Work even until 38 rnds have been completed. Fasten off.

Brim: With contrasting color, ch 13. *Row 1:* Sc in 2nd ch from hook and in each ch across—12 sc; ch 1, turn. *Row 2:* Working in back lp of each st across, sc in 2nd st from hook and in each st across; ch 1, turn. Rep Row 2 until the length of the brim equals the circumference of the crown at the lower edge. Fasten off. Sew short ends of brim tog. Sew 1 long edge of brim to lower edge of crown; roll brim.

Crocheted Scarf

Finished size is 6x54 inches, excluding fringe.

▬▬▬ HOW TO ▬▬▬

Materials
Small amounts of the following colors of Coats and Clark Red Heart 4-ply hand-knitting yarn: amethyst, skipper blue, paddy green, yellow, vibrant orange, jockey red, and off-white
Size I aluminum crochet hook, or size to obtain gauge

Gauge: 4 sc = 1 inch.
Abbreviations: See page 214.

Instructions

With amethyst, ch 217. *Row 1:* Sc in 2nd ch from hook and in each ch across—216 sc; ch 1, turn. *Row 2:* Sc in each sc across; drop amethyst, pick up blue by pulling new color through last lp made; turn. Rep Row 2, changing colors after every 2 rows and

working in the following color sequence: green, yellow, orange, red, off-white, red, orange, yellow, green, blue, amethyst. Fasten off.

Fringe: Cut eight 12-inch lengths of off-white and sixteen 12-inch lengths of rem colors. Using 4 strands at a time, knot a grp of fringe at the end of matching-color row. Trim ends.

Knitted Stocking Cap

Instructions are for small size; changes for sizes medium and large follow in parentheses.

▬▬▬ HOW TO ▬▬▬

Materials
1 skein (3.5 ounces) of Coats and Clark Red Heart 4-ply hand-knitting yarn in color of your choice
Small amount of off-white yarn for pompon
Knitting needles in sizes 6 and 8, or sizes to obtain gauge
Yarn needle

Gauge: With larger needles over st st, 4 sts = 1 inch; 6 rows = 1 inch.
Abbreviations: See page 212.

Instructions

With smaller needles, cast on 70 (80, 90) sts. Work in k 1, p 1 ribbing for 1¼ (1½, 1½) inches. Change to larger needles and work even in st st until work measures 8½ (9, 9½) inches, ending with a p row.

Top shaping: Row 1: *K 2 tog. Rep from * across. *Row 2:* P. *Row 3:* Rep Row 1. Break yarn, leaving a 30-in. tail. Thread needle with tail and draw through rem sts on needle and pull tight to form crown. Sew back seams with tail, matching rows.

Pompon: Wrap a 4-inch-wide cardboard strip with off-white yarn 75 times. Sl the yarn off the cardboard and tie it in the center of the bundle. Clip the loops on the ends; fluff the yarn to shape the pompon. Trim the ends if necessary. Tack to crown. Fold back brim.

Knitted Scarf

Finished size is 9 inches wide.

━━━HOW TO━━━

Materials
1 skein Coats and Clark Red Heart 4-ply hand-knitting

yarn (3.5 ounces) in the following colors: **red, orange, yellow, green, blue, violet**
Size 8 knitting needles, or size to obtain gauge

Gauge: Over garter stitch, 4 sts = 1 inch; 10 rows = 1 inch.
Continued

Abbreviations: See page 212.

Instructions

With red, cast on 36 sts. Work even in garter st (k each row) for 10 rows. Change to orange; work even in garter st for 10 rows. Working 10 rows of each color, establish rem stripe sequence as follows: yellow, green, blue, and violet. Change to red and rep 6-color stripe sequence 7 times more, ending with violet. Cast off.

Knitted Mittens

Instructions are for children's sizes 2-4. Changes for children's sizes 6-8 and 10-12, and for women's size medium and men's size medium follow in parentheses.

▰▰▰ HOW TO ▰▰▰

Materials

1 skein (3.5 ounces) of Coats and Clark Red Heart 4-ply hand-knitting yarn in any color
Knitting needles in sizes 5 and 7, or any size to obtain gauge

Gauge: With larger needles over st st, 5 sts = 1 inch; 6 rows = 1 inch.

Abbreviations: See page 212.

Instructions

Right mitten: With smaller needles cast on 21 (25, 29, 33, 37) sts. Work in k 1, p 1 ribbing for 1½ (2, 2½, 2½, 2½) inches. Change to the larger needles. *Next row:* K across, inc 6 sts evenly spaced—27 (31, 35, 39, 43) sts. *Following row:* P. Now work even in st st until 4 (4, 4, 6, 6) rows have been worked above ribbing.

Thumb gusset: Row 1: K 13 (15, 17, 19, 21), inc 1 st in each of next 2 sts, k 12 (14, 16, 18, 20). *Row 2:* P. *Row 3:* K 13 (15, 17, 19, 21), inc 1 st in next st, k 2, inc 1 st in next st, k 12 (14, 16, 18, 20) sts. *Row 4:* P. *For sizes 6-8, 10-12, women's, and men's only: Row 5:* K (15, 17, 19, 21), inc 1 st in next st, k 4, inc 1 st in next st, k (14, 16, 18, 20). *Row 6:* P. *For sizes 10-12, women's, and men's only: Row 7:* K (17, 19, 21), inc 1 st in next st, k 6, inc 1 st in next st, k (16, 18, 20). *Row 8:* P. *For men's size only: Row 9:* K (21), inc 1 st in next st, k 8, inc 1 st in next st, k (20). *Row 10:* P. *All sizes: Next row:* K 13 (15, 17, 19, 21) sts, inc 1 st in next st, k 6 (8, 10, 10, 12) sts, inc 1 st in next st, k 12 (14, 16, 18, 20). *Following row:* P.

Thumb: K 13 (15, 17, 19, 21), sl sts on right-hand needle to holder, k 8 (10, 12, 12, 14) sts across thumb; sl rem 12 (14, 16, 18, 20) sts to holder. Work in st st over 8 (10, 12, 12, 14) sts for 7 (9, 11, 13, 15) rows more. *Next row:* * K 2 tog. Rep from * across—5 (5, 6, 6, 7) sts. Cut off yarn, leaving a 15-inch tail. Thread yarn needle with tail and draw through rem sts; draw up tightly. Turn the thumb to the wrong side and sew end and seam securely. Turn the thumb right side out.

Hand: Sl sts on holder to right of thumb to right needle; sl sts on holder to left of thumb to left needle. K across sts on left needle—25 (29, 33, 37, 41) sts. Work even in st st for 13 (17, 19, 23, 25) rows more. Now dec for tip of mitten as follows: *Row 1:* K 2 tog, k 1, k 2 tog, * k 2, k 2 tog. Rep from * across. *Row 2:* P. *Row 3:* * K 1, k 2 tog. Rep from * across. *Row 4:* P. *Row 5:* * K 2 tog. Rep from * across.

Cut off sufficient yarn to sew the seam. Cast off sts and finish the main seam, tying off and weaving in the yarn ends.

Make the Left Mitten in the same manner, reversing shaping around thumb gusset.

Tips for stitchers

Is one of these knitted sweaters or accessories going to be your first knitting project? If so, follow these handy pointers and your beginning attempt should be a great success.
• **Match gauge carefully:** The instructions for most knitted or crocheted garments and accessories include a *gauge*, which is the number of stitches and rows per inch. To avoid poorly fitting and unsuccessful garments, make sure that the printed gauge is identical to the gauge you are creating with yarn and needles or hook.

Before beginning a project, knit or crochet a small swatch with the yarn and needles or hook you intend to use. Then measure the number of stitches and rows per inch. If the number of stitches is less than the number printed, switch to a smaller needle or hook; if the number of stitches is more than the number printed, switch to a larger needle or hook. Adjust all the other needle or hook sizes accordingly.
• **Read instructions carefully:** Glance through the instructions from beginning to end before starting to knit or crochet. If there are unfamiliar techniques, ask a friend who knits or crochets, or someone at a yarn shop, to instruct you.
• **Block pieces correctly:** Before assembling a knitted or crocheted garment or accessory, block the pieces. Dampen each piece with cool water, then pin the pieces out onto a padded surface, such as double layers of bath towels or a plywood board covered with felt sheeting. Using rustproof pins, carefully pin the dampened pieces to the towels or board. Let the pieces dry away from heat and direct sunlight.

Striped Socks

Small skeins of leftover yarns are also the starting point for these snazzy striped socks. They're knitted the traditional way, on four double-pointed needles. You can vary the stripe pattern according to whim and the amounts and colors of yarn you have on hand. If the yarn supply is plentiful, you might want to extend these short sport socks into knee socks by simply lengthening the leg.

═══HOW TO═══

Materials
Bits and pieces of leftover knitting worsted yarn in desired colors. Or, 1 skein (4 ounces) each of Bernat Berella 4 (4-ply knitting worsted yarn) in the following colors: scarlet (A), white (B), black (C), rose (D), and gold (E)

1 set of size 4 double-pointed knitting needles, or size to obtain gauge below

Gauge: 6 sts = 1 inch; 15 rnds = 2 inches.

Abbreviations: See page 212.

Instructions
Beg at cuff with A, cast on 48 sts. Divide sts evenly over 3 needles, taking care not to twist or drop sts. Place a marker on needle to mark beg of rnd. Work in k 2, p 2 ribbing for 12 rnds.

Leg: K 1 rnd in A. Work even in st st (k each rnd), working 5 rnds each of B, C, D, C, E, A, B, and C—41 rnds.

With C, k first 11 sts of rnd, sl last 23 sts worked to a dp needle for heel; hold rem 25 sts on 2 needles for instep.

Heel: Use color C throughout.
Row 1 (wrong side): Sl first st as if to p; p to end.

Row 2: Sl first st as if to p; k to end. Rpt last 2 rows until 14 rows of heel have been completed, ending with Row 2.

Turn the heel as follows: Sl 1, p 13, p 2 tog, p 1, turn; sl 1, k 6, sl 1, k 1, psso, k 1, turn; sl 1, p 7, p 2 tog, p 1, turn; sl 1, k 8, sl 1, k 1, psso, k 1, turn; sl 1, p 9, p 2 tog, p 1, turn. Work toward sides of heel, with 1 st more before dec on each row, until 15 sts rem.

Gussets and foot: Pick up and k 8 sts along the side of the heel and place on 1 needle; sl and k 25 sts from instep to 1 needle; pick up and k 8 st on other side of heel and place on 1 needle—41 sts.

Rnd 1: With C, k around.
Rnd 2: K to within 3 sts to end of first needle, k 2 tog, k 1; k across instep needle; k 1, sl 1, k 1, psso, k to end of rnd on third needle.
Rnd 3: Change to D, k around.
Rnd 4: With D, rpt Rnd 2.
Rnd 5: K around.

Rnd 6: Rpt Rnd 2.
Rnd 7: K around.
Rnd 8: Change to C; rpt Rnd 2.

Work even in rnds, work 4 more rnds of C; then work 5 rnds of each color in this sequence: E, A, B, C, D, C, and E.

Divide the rem sts as follows: 12 sts on the first needle, 24 sts on the second needle, 12 sts on the third needle.

Toe: (Use color A throughout.)
Dec rnd: K to within 3 sts of end of first needle, k 2 tog, k 1; on second needle k 1, sl 1, k 1, psso, k to within 3 sts of end, k 2 tog, k 1; on third needle k 1, sl 1, k 1, psso, k to end. *Next rnd:* Work even.

Rpt last 2 rnds 5 times more; then rpt dec rnd every rnd until 12 sts rem. K 3 sts of first needle and sl to third needle. Weave sole and instep sts together.

Work other sock to match.

Making Yarn Substitutions

Knitted and crocheted projects are usually designed with a specific yarn in mind. Although pattern instructions may be flexible in regard to the choice of color, other characteristics of the yarn (such as weight, texture, and elasticity) are often essential to the character of the finished garment.

The appeal of a high-fashion sweater, for example, may depend on the cloudlike texture of a mohair yarn or the artful use of glittery metallic threads. As a general rule of thumb, then, the surest way to duplicate the look of a garment in a pattern book is to follow the list of materials, specifications, and instructions to the letter.

However, if you're adventuresome and have scrap yarn, or if you can't find the yarn called for in the pattern, there are ways to make the most of what you have on hand.

To decide whether you can substitute one yarn (or a combination of yarns) for the materials called for in a given pattern, keep in mind the pattern style, type of yarn, and—most important—gauge.

Pattern Style

Scale of the project should be your first consideration. If you have just 4 or 5 half-skeins of assorted leftover yarns, think of small projects such as hats, scarves, or mittens. But if your supply of scrap yarn is more extensive, you may wish to settle on a more ambitious project.

Whatever you decide to make, select a pattern that is not dominated by or dependent on a specific yarn. In other words, don't expect to reproduce the look of a knitted chenille jacket with dimestore acrylic yarn! If the yarn you want to use has unusual characteristics of its own, look for a pattern that will make the most of its bulk, texture, or other qualities.

If you plan to combine several different colors and/or textures of yarn scraps into one project, select a simple pattern, such as a crewneck sweater worked in stripes or a patchwork scarf or afghan, so that the mixture of colors and/or textures will not compete with or obscure the original lines or stitch pattern of the design.

Interchangeable Yarns

Excluding novelty materials such as bouclés or thick-and-thin yarns, most of the yarns used for knitted and crocheted projects, depending on their thickness, can be divided into four basic categories by weight or size. The categories are baby or fingering yarn, sport, knitting worsted-weight, and bulky.

Fingering yarn (or baby yarn) is the finest, and is used for baby items, socks, and fine knits. Sport yarn is primarily for adults' and children's apparel. Knitting worsted yarns are used for garments and home accessories, and bulky yarns are popular for quick-knit sweaters, caps, and scarves.

In general, you can successfully substitute wool, acrylic, or blended yarns that fall into the same category for each other in most patterns, even though they may have different textures or come from different manufacturers. It is *not* advisable, though, to substitute cotton, linen, or metallics for wool yarns. Because these fibers lack wool's springiness and elasticity, a substitution will invariably affect the shape and fit of the garment.

If pattern instructions list a brand name of yarn, but fail to give the generic category (such as ''sport weight'' or ''bulky''), you can determine the type of yarn required by comparing the gauge and suggested needle/crochet hook size with the following chart.

Baby or fingering yarn:
Gauge: 7 sts = 1 inch
Needle/Hook size: 3-5/D

Sport:
Gauge: 6 sts = 1 inch
Needle/Hook size: 5/F-G

Worsted:
Gauge: 5 sts = 1 inch
Needle/Hook size: 8-10/H-I

Bulky:
Gauge: 7 sts = 2 inches
Needle/Hook size: 10-13/K

Identifying the basic category of yarn called for in a pattern will give you a general idea of what sorts of yarns are suitable for the design. However, the most important step in determining whether two yarns are interchangeable is to work up a swatch to gauge.

Gauge

Knit and crochet instructions always include a gauge, which is a precise measurement of the number of stitches for each inch of width and for the number of rows for each vertical inch in the knitted or crocheted fabric of the completed project. All directions are based on the given gauge, as this controls the size and shape of the finished piece. To duplicate the designer's results, *you must work exactly to the gauge.*

Gauge is influenced by three factors: the size or weight of the yarn used, the size of the needles or crochet hook with which you work, and the tension at which you stitch. Tension—or the stress you exert on the yarn as you work—varies widely from person to person. Even if you're using precisely the same yarn and the same size hook or needles as those recommended in the directions, your gauge may well differ from that required for the successful completion of the pattern.

To test the gauge, work up a sample swatch with the yarn and hook or needles you plan to use. Cast on or chain enough stitches so that your swatch measures approximately 4 inches wide. Then work in the pattern stitch described in the instructions until the swatch is approximately 4 inches square.

Remove your swatch from the needles or hook, smooth it out, and pin it to a flat surface. Take measurements in the middle of the swatch where the tension is likely to be most even. To do this, place two straight pins exactly 2 inches apart horizontally in the middle of the swatch. Count the number of stitches between the pins; repeat the measurement vertically.

If your stitch count matches the given gauge, you're ready to start the project. If you have too many stitches per inch, switch to slightly larger knitting needles or crochet hook. If you have too few stitches, use a smaller hook or pair of needles. One stitch—even a half-stitch—out of gauge may not seem significant on a 4-inch swatch, but over an entire garment, it can make a drastic difference in size, fit, and general appearance.

If you take the time to check your gauge carefully, any yarn that can be knitted or crocheted to match the required gauge can be substituted for the specified yarn.

Keep in mind, though, that in striving to match a given gauge, the size of the needles or hook you use should not vary more than a size or two from that suggested in the instructions. The look of the pattern stitch may change drastically if you deviate too widely from the pattern's recommended size of hook or needles and the suggested weight yarn.

Amount of Yarn

Yarns are usually packaged according to weight. Most American yarns are weighed in ounces, while many imported yarns are measured by grams.

Pattern instructions often call for a given number of "1-ounce skeins" or "50-gram balls" of a specific yarn. If you substitute another yarn and want to determine how many balls or skeins you need, the conversion chart below listing common amounts of yarn and their *approximate* ounce-gram equivalents may prove helpful.

However, remember that the final determinant for the amount of yarn required for any project is actually yardage, rather than weight. Equal weights of equivalent yarns will have *roughly* equivalent yardage, but when in doubt, always count on an extra skein.

1 ounce = approximately 28 grams

40 grams = approximately 1⅓ ounces

50 grams = approximately 1¾ ounces

100 grams = approximately 3½ ounces

Mixing Yarns

Most patterns call for a single type of yarn to be used throughout the project. But if you don't have enough of an appropriate yarn, there are a number of imaginative alternatives open to you.

First, you might combine two or more strands of a lighter weight yarn to approximate the weight of a heavier yarn. For example, use two strands of sport or worsted to make up a bulky yarn.

It's not necessary for the two strands to be the same color or even the same type. Try mixing a variety of solid-color yarns with a continuous strand of white for a tweedy, crayon-colored effect (see the sweaters on page 104 and the crocheted afghan on page 83).

Stripes—random or in a repetitive pattern—are another way to use up small amounts of similar-weight yarns in many colors. Any design worked in a plain stockinette stitch (see the sport socks on page 113) adapts well to stripes.

For other projects, try experimenting with a neutral or monochromatic color scheme, mixing different shades of one color or different textures within a single

shade. This technique works well in striped or patchwork patterns.

Using small amounts of more exotic yarns for collars, cuffs, borders, or trim is another way to stretch a too-short supply of yarn into a complete project.

A word of warning: In most cases, it is advisable to mix only those fibers that can be cleaned in the same way. If any one type of yarn used in a project has to be dry-cleaned, the entire garment will have to be cleaned that way.

Mixed Media

Some of the most fashionable clothes on today's market are artful combinations of several craft techniques. For instance, there are knitted sweaters with quilted patchwork fronts, and wool-plaid jackets with crocheted, chubby sleeves. Whether you begin such a garment from scratch or decide to piece together parts salvaged from clothing that is past its prime, this trend is a scrap crafter's dream.

Study fashion magazines and browse through your favorite stores for ideas on how to combine your own skills and scraps into a high-fashion look at a low price.

Recycling Yarn

If you have a garment made of beautiful yarn, but find the item is no longer wearable, reclaim the yarn for use in another project. Unravel the yarn, winding it into a large skein. Holding onto the end of the yarn, wind it around your elbow, then back between thumb and forefinger.

Continue winding until it is about the size of a skein of knitting worsted. Lay it flat; tie a strand of yarn loosely around the skein in several places to prevent it from tangling.

Immerse the skein in water until it is completely saturated. Wrap it in a towel and squeeze out the excess moisture. Stretch the skein over the back of a chair and let it dry completely. Then, if the yarn is still kinky, repeat the process.

FROM THE
Children's Gallery

From tots to teens, kids of all ages seem to have a natural talent for scrap crafts. And they bring such zest and imagination to every undertaking that the results are almost always special, no matter what they're making.

Whether the kids tackle these projects on their own or need an occasional hand from an encouraging adult, you'll find plenty of ideas here to engage their imagination. What's more, they'll find the fun is often as much in the making as it is in enjoying the finished project!

For instance, consider the delightful block town shown here. Older children can paint their fantasies directly onto scrap lumber, or generously help to immortalize the doodles of a younger brother or sister by tracing their drawings and transferring them to wood.

For more ways to translate kids' drawings into unique gifts and toys, please turn the page.

Puppets, Pillows, and Playthings

With a splash of paint or a stitch from your needle, you can turn kids' drawings into treasured gifts and playthings like those shown here and on pages 116-117.

Block Town

HOW TO

Materials
Wood scraps, sandpaper
Tracing paper and carbon or graphite paper
Acrylic paints, brushes
Clear acrylic varnish

Instructions

Collect a small child's drawings of neighborhood landmarks, then select scrap lumber in corresponding shapes and sizes. Sand the scraps smooth and paint them white or bright primary colors.

Trace outlines of drawings onto tracing paper; transfer to wood using carbon or graphite paper. Paint with acrylics and varnish when dry.

Dolls and Puppets

Children love to draw their friends and family members, and with a little appliqué and embroidery, you can turn these pictures into special "portrait" dolls and puppets.

HOW TO

Materials
Scraps of muslin, felt, and colorful print fabrics
Fusible webbing
Zigzag sewing machine
Thread and embroidery floss

Instructions

Enlarge and simplify your child's drawing, if necessary, then transfer the outlines to muslin using dressmaker's carbon paper.

Cut the clothing and hair shapes from colorful fabrics and secure the pieces to muslin with fusible webbing.

Machine-satin stitch around the appliqués; add faces and other details with hand or machine embroidery or fabric markers.

• **For dolls,** cut out the body shape and satin stitch it to a black felt backing, leaving an opening for stuffing. Stuff the doll, sew the opening closed, then trim the felt backing. Leave about ¼ inch of felt bordering the toy to look like the outlines of the original drawing.

• **For hand puppets,** adapt the drawing to a simple mitt or hand-puppet shape, large enough to fit over a child's hand. Appliqué the portrait shape to a felt backing, but leave the bottom open and hem straight across.

Pillows

HOW TO

Instructions

To capture a prized picture in needlework, trace the drawing onto muslin or solid-color fabric with a water-soluble embroidery pen. Using the original drawing as a guide, re-create the picture in appliqué, embroidery, and quilting. Sew into a pillow.

Kitchen Cover-Ups

Could your kitchen use a little brightening? If so, ask a willing youngster to help. Put pen and paper into his hands and a few objects on the table for him to draw. In a jiffy, you'll have lots of youthful, fresh drawings to translate into fabric appliqués for these colorful appliance covers, right.

Your enthusiastic young designer may want to assist with the cooking, too. So dash off an extra-special apron for your child-artist-turned-cook. Use his or her drawings to pep up a ready-made apron or fashion your own from a remnant.

HOW TO

Materials
Crayons or felt pens
White paper, tissue paper
Fabric scraps in various colors
    and patterns
Fabric glue or fusible webbing
Sewing threads
Piping, seam binding
Purchased apron or fabric
    remnant

Instructions
Give your youngster crayons or felt-tip pens and paper. Suggest that he or she use black for outlines and colors for filling in the shapes, so designs may be interpreted easily when cutting them from fabric.

For kitchen designs like ours, provide the child with objects to draw. Place simple objects on the table first. Ask him or her to draw an apple, a banana, grapes, and a pear. After a few drawings are finished, ask him to draw your toaster or blender. If the drawings are small you can enlarge them by using a grid enlarging procedure. From the drawings, make tissue paper patterns for appliqués.

• **For the toaster and blender covers,** cut fronts, backs, and side panels that fit your toaster and blender using quilted fabric.

Cut fruit or appliance shapes from colored fabrics, using tissue paper patterns.

Attach appliqués to quilted fabric fronts of toaster and blender covers with fabric glue or fusible webbing. With your sewing machine set on a medium-width zig-zag stitch, sew around the raw edges of each appliqué. For narrow lines (stems, cords), use lines of satin stitching.

Next, stitch contrasting piping around raw edges of toaster and blender fronts and backs. With right sides facing, sew center panels between the fronts and backs along previous stitching lines. Trim seams, clip curves, and turn the covers right side out. Finish bottoms with narrow hems or additional piping.

• **For the apron,** machine appliqué the child's drawings as you do for the appliance covers. To make apron from scratch, measure width of child and length of area you wish to cover to determine the dimensions of fabric needed. Cut a rectangle this size from fabric. Fold the material in half lengthwise with right sides together. Using the photograph as a guide, carefully cut a gentle curve from one of the outside corners of the folded rectangle to create the bib section.

Make a ½-inch hem along the straight sides and bottom of apron. Use bias tape to protect edges of apron top and curves; stitch bias tape to top of apron. Create apron ties, neck piece, and edges of curved sections from one long piece of bias tape. (Center of piece should be at back of neck.) Stitch curves first, then stitch neck and ties closed.

Adapting Kids' Art to Needlework

Children's spontaneous doodles and drawings provide a delightfully personal source of design ideas for almost every craft technique—from needlepoint to stained glass. Moreover, kids' young-at-art sense of color, line, and perspective has a freshness and originality that makes more conventional designs seem stale and unimaginative in comparison.

To help you translate your youngsters' artistic efforts into more durable mementos, here are a few valuable suggestions on how to adapt original artwork to be used as patterns for craft projects.

Selecting and Adapting Designs

If you don't already have on hand enough raw material, such as salvaged scribbles and carefully saved classroom drawings, or if you want to gather drawings on a specific theme for use with a particular project, here are several simple techniques you can use to guide your children in making drawings that will translate effectively into craft designs.

First of all, provide the young artists with a good selection of crayons and/or wide-tip felt pens. Suggest that they use black or dark colors for outlines and lighter, more vibrant colors for filling in the designs. This will encourage strong, well-defined shapes that are easiest to reproduce in some media—such as fabric appliqué or stained glass.

If you have a particular project in mind (squares for a baby quilt, for example, or small motifs for a series of block-print cards), suggest that the kids work to the scale that suits your project. You might give them sheets of paper to work on that are the size and shape of the designs you require. But also remember that enlarging all or a portion of any picture can produce wonderfully bold, dramatic results. If the drawings you intend to use are too small as they are, enlarge them for use as patterns. (Refer to pages 78-79 for suggestions on enlarging and reducing designs.)

Preserving Original Artwork

Most kids' finest artistic efforts end up on comparatively flimsy newsprint, which is often used in art classes. Newsprint tends to crease, yellow, and tear easily. To preserve pictures until you are ready to work from them, store the drawings rolled around cardboard tubes, or store them flat in a box, with pieces of tissue paper sandwiched between the designs. If folded, the pictures will eventually crack and tear along the creases.

To keep pictures out and on display, mount drawings or paintings on pieces of colorful poster board and cover them with a protective sheet of clear, adhesive-backed plastic. Or slip smaller pictures into purchased plastic sleeves to make a set of wipe-clean place mats. Change or rotate pictures on a regular basis to display "new works by the artist" or to reflect changing seasonal interests.

Also use children's artwork "as is" to embellish all sorts of everyday household surfaces, such as inexpensive metal wastebaskets, notebooks, and trays. Just affix the picture with adhesive spray or rubber cement, then protect with several coats of clear acrylic spray or a layer of clear, adhesive-backed plastic. Using your thumb or a printmaker's brayer (available at art supply stores), remove any air bubbles between the picture and plastic covering so you're sure to have a tight, durable bond.

Any picture that you intend to use as a pattern for a project should be protected by a sheet of clear acetate or clear adhesive-backed plastic to preserve the original from harm. Then, when you've stitched the design into a rug or used it as the central motif of an appliquéd quilt, just frame and hang the original design near your crafty adaptation.

Needlepoint

Children's naive drawings often seem surprisingly sophisticated once they're interpreted in needlepoint. Even the simplest, most ingenuous depiction of "My Mother with Flowers" or "My Dog, Spot" assumes the quality of a contemporary folk art design when it's stitched on canvas.

If necessary, when making a pattern from original artwork, eliminate extraneous details for the sake of balance or composition, or pull out and focus on one single element of the drawing to be enlarged and worked in needlepoint. Transfer the pattern to a large sheet of sturdy paper and go over lines of the design with a heavy black marking pen.

Slip the paper pattern under a piece of needlepoint canvas and trace the outlines of the design onto the canvas with a permanent needlepoint canvas marker. You can work your design on any size needlepoint canvas you choose, though it will be easiest to see and trace the pattern through a No. 10- or No. 12-count mono canvas or a large-mesh rug canvas.

For a canvas that's to be the same size as the original drawing, simply place a piece of clear acetate over the drawing to protect it, and then slip the drawing under the canvas and trace. Always be careful not to damage the original artwork if you want to frame and hang it later.

When choosing yarns to stitch your needlepoint picture, you may wish to lighten or brighten some of the colors used in the original drawing for the sake of contrast. But do try to stay as close to the original as possible. A child's use of color is often highly original, and blue dogs and purple people are part of the fun of this sort of enterprise.

Once the design is sketched onto the canvas, outline each separate area or color block in continental stitches. Fill the large areas of color with basket-weave or novelty stitches of your choice.

Block Prints

The bold lines and chunky shapes of kids' line drawings have a graphic impact that is ideal for a block print image. Select a single strong shape as the basis for the design—perhaps a simple stick figure, a tree, a flower, or the outline of a car or animal.

If you plan to print the design as a repeat pattern on paper or fabric, trace over it several times in a row on a sheet of paper, just to get an idea of how the image works in multiple repeats. You may find it necessary to broaden the actual lines of the design, for example, or to eliminate certain details.

To set up your print shop, you'll need small linoleum blocks and a selection of carving tools (available through craft, hobby, and art supply stores). You'll also need several sheets of carbon paper, a printer's brayer or soft paintbrush, and a supply of acrylic or fabric paint. If small hands are to be involved in the printing process, stick with water-soluble poster paints for simple prints (and easy cleanup).

There are several ways to approach the design adaptation. First, center and trace the shape you've chosen onto the linoleum surface. Use carbon or graphite paper to transfer the design, and be careful to trace the shape *in reverse* on the linoleum. Because the print will be a mirror image of the design carved on the block, you need to flop the design before carving it, so the final printed image will be exactly as the young artist originally drew it.

There are two different ways to carve the block into a usable printing surface. One is to gouge out all the material around the actual outlines of the design. The design lines should remain at least ⅛ inch wide to ensure a clean, bold print. When the block is inked and pressed onto paper or fabric, this technique will result in a positive image—that is, a colored-line print of the design.

For a negative image, carefully carve out just the actual lines of the design itself. Then, when the block is inked and printed, the image will appear as a white outline on a solid field of color.

Once the linoleum block—or set of blocks—is carved, it can be used over and over again to print anything from kitchen curtains to party invitations.

To print on fabric, first spread out the prewashed and pressed fabric on a pad of newspapers (to blot excess paint if it seeps through the fabric). Apply a thin, even coat of acrylic or fabric paint to the design surface of the block with a brayer or paintbrush. Apply the block to fabric with a smooth, even pressure, then lift the block straight up again. To avoid smudges, do not slide or jiggle the block.

Reink the block for each print, and wipe the block clean after every third or fourth print—or whenever the linoleum becomes caked or tacky. When the paint dries, follow the manufacturer's directions to heat-set the designs on the wrong side of the fabric.

To print on paper or cardboard, use acrylics or poster paints and follow the same inking and printing procedures described above. You might also experiment with colored, preinked stamp pads, if the linoleum block is small enough to fit on the surface of the stamp pad.

Children, too, can get involved in block print projects, but *it's best to keep sharp linoleum carving tools out of small hands.* For a very young printmaker, ask adults or older children to carve out a block from the youngster's designs, then allow the child to transfer the block print to paper.

Appliqué and Embroidery

Fabric interpretations of children's drawings offer unique design possibilities for both clothing and home furnishings projects. As described in the instructions for pillows and other appliqué projects on page 118, just cut basic shapes from fabric and fuse them to a background material. Then add details and embellishments using hand or machine embroidery with a touch or two of quilting.

The project possibilities are endless. You might turn a series of small pictures into appliquéd squares for a child's quilt, or stitch the fabric version of a favorite drawing onto the front of a school knapsack or the back of a denim jacket. Embroider single design elements—flowers, birds, or small figures—on a collar, a pocket, a baby's bib, or anywhere a bit of embellishment seems appropriate.

Other Applications

Once you begin to look at children's drawings in terms of possible project designs, you'll keep finding new and inventive ways to interpret the youngsters' artwork in your own favorite craft techniques.

Consider using the designs for glass, pottery, fabric-painted T-shirts, woodburned lamp bases, batiked scarves, painted designs on wooden furniture, dolls, and toys, to name just a few applications. You're sure to think of hundreds more.

Crayon Crafts

Young artists love to see their works on display—and the creative projects on these two pages have been specially designed to showcase the talents of the crayon set!

Life-Size Portraits

Why not commission a collection of life-size portraits of friends and family from your own poster-paint Picassos and their pals? Then exhibit the finished portraits in a garage or family room and invite the neighborhood over for a rogues' gallery preview!

HOW TO

Materials

Wide rolls of butcher paper or newsprint
Washable marking pens
Poster paints, brushes
Crayons

Instructions

Invite one child to lie flat on his back on a large sheet of paper. The next child then traces an outline of his or her friend on the paper with a marking pen, carefully following the contours of the body. (Parents might lend a helping hand here, if the kids have any trouble sketching wiggling bodies.)

Next, lay out a second sheet of paper and have the children switch places. Continue until each child working on the project has an outline of himself, a friend, or family member to color.

Now children can complete the portraits, filling in the outlines with poster paints, markers, or crayons. Encourage each child to make his portrait as realistic or as fanciful as he likes.

Finished portraits might be displayed in a neighborhood gallery, or each child can keep his portrait for home display.

It also can be glued to a piece of hardboard or plywood, equipped with hooks, and mounted on an easel stand to be used as a valet on which to hang clothing in the child's room.

Colorful Crayon Bedspread

Here's a whimsical way to preserve a selection of your child's early artistic efforts. Motifs on the bedspread are created with fabric crayons (available at art and crafts stores), and transferred to sheet fabric with a touch of the iron.

═══════HOW TO═══════

Materials
White or light-colored, polyester-blend sheet
Matching pillow cases
Set of Crayola fabric crayons
Large sheets of drawing paper
Iron

Instructions

First mark small squares of each crayon color on a sheet of paper and transfer this "test sheet" to a scrap of fabric. (Polyester-blend fabrics take color best; dye will print on all-cotton fabric, but colors are less brilliant and may fade when washed.) This test piece will give you an idea of how colors look when transferred to fabric; they are much more intense than they appear on paper.

Next, encourage your resident young artist to make a series of drawings on his or her favorite theme (spacemen, dinosaurs, flowers, etc.). Make drawings on large sheets of paper, then transfer designs to fabric, following directions on the crayon package.

Spread sheet fabric on a layer of newspapers, place one drawing facedown on the fabric. then cover with a piece of clean white paper. Set iron on cotton setting and press with a steady, strong pressure over the entire design, until the color becomes slightly visible through the top sheet of paper. Once the design is transferred to synthetic-blend fabric, the color print is washable and permanent.

Of course you don't have to tackle an entire bedspread to test this technique. A couple of pillow tops, a border for bedroom curtains, or a set of place mats and napkins are equally pleasing ways to preserve your children's favorite pictures.

One thing to keep in mind: pictures print in *reverse* on the fabric. If you want to include a name or message in your design, write or trace the letters backward on the paper so the words print legibly.

"Handmade" Gifts

Homemade gifts always have a special charm—and a special meaning to those lucky enough to receive them. Best of all, the "loving-hands" touches on the gifts shown here and on pages 128-129 are a great way to get kids involved in the fun of gift making and giving!

Apron

═══HOW TO═══

Materials
¾ yard of muslin
Scrap of red fabric for heart
1½ yards of wide red bias tape
3 yards of red hem facing
1½ yards of 6-inch-wide ruffled eyelet
Red, water-soluble textile ink or fabric paint
Red embroidery floss
Printmaker's brayer

Instructions

Enlarge the apron pattern, opposite, and transfer it to muslin. Plan the position of the handprints (one for each child).

Squeeze ink or paint onto a flat surface (such as a cookie sheet) and roll it into a smooth, sticky surface with the brayer. Brush paint or ink onto hands or roll it onto hands with the brayer.

Immediately press hands onto fabric, rolling palm and fingers slightly to form a complete imprint. Refer to manufacturer's instructions (on paint or ink package) for setting the color.

Next, use light pencil to write names beneath handprints and to sketch in a message. Embroider names and message with three strands of floss in stem stitches. Appliqué the heart in place.

Bind the lower edge of the apron with bias tape and add eyelet trim. Use hem facing to bind the top and sides of the apron and to make the neck strap and ties.

"Hand" Bag

═══HOW TO═══

Materials
23x35-inch piece of canvas and matching piece of lining fabric
Red, water-soluble textile ink or fabric paint
Printmaker's brayer
Embroidery floss

Instructions

Enlarge the tote pattern, opposite, and transfer it to canvas and lining fabric. Cut bag and strap

pieces from both fabrics. Print and embroider front of tote, following directions for printing and embroidering apron, above.

Fold large canvas piece in half crosswise (right sides facing). Beginning 1½ inches above the fold, stitch along sides (¼-inch seams). Flatten the bottom of the bag along the fold; sew across side seams to make a flat bottom. Repeat with the lining piece.

Line straps, leaving wide end open on each for turning. Turn straps, press, and topstitch with contrasting thread. Stitch the wide end of one strap to each side of the bag. Slip lining into the bag (wrong

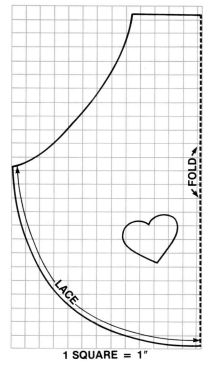

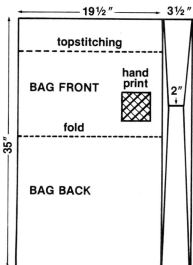

sides together), turn under raw edges, pin, and stitch in place. Press top edge and topstitch in contrasting thread to finish. Knot straps together as shown above.

Potholder and Dish Towel

=====HOW TO=====

Instructions

For the potholder, make a handprint on a 10-inch square of muslin. Back with thick batting and a second square of muslin, then quilt around the printed shape by hand or machine. Bind with bias tape and add a loop for hanging.

For a matching dish towel, print a plain, purchased towel, embroider a homey message, and trim with bias tape and eyelet.

FOLD

LACE

1 SQUARE = 1″

◄——— 19½ ″ ———► 3½ ″

topstitching

BAG FRONT   hand print   2″

fold

35″

BAG BACK

continued

The sprightly red and white coverlet, opposite, is a splendid and very personalized rendition of an out-of-the-ordinary family tree. And it's easy to create—a simple design with machine-appliquéd tree and heart motifs—but the crowning touches are the handprints, representing every member of the family.

To print your family's hands, plan a work session around a special occasion, such as a reunion or a holiday dinner. Or mail off kits of fabric, ink, and careful instructions to faraway relatives if you want to include all family members on the quilt.

Instructions below are for a double-bed-size coverlet, but they easily can be adapted to fit any size bed.

HOW TO

Materials
Six 25-inch squares of good-quality muslin fabric (approximately 4½ yards of muslin)
Red, water-soluble textile ink or fabric paint
2 yards of red polka-dot fabric
Polyester fiberfill
Red cotton lining fabric, pieced to measure 48x72 inches
5 yards of 44/45-inch-wide red quilted fabric for borders
Red and maroon fabric scraps for leaves and hearts
Red embroidery floss
Embroidery needle and hoop
5½ yards of red, wide bias tape
5½ yards of 2½-inch-wide pregathered eyelet lace
Printmaker's brayer

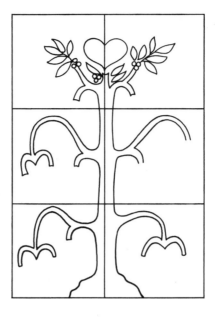

Instructions
To plan your quilt, refer to the pattern for a family with four children, above right. If you have fewer—or more—offspring in your family, add or subtract branches as necessary. Plan to have parents' handprints toward the top of the tree, children's prints on lower branches. Put the children's hands in descending order of age and add any grandchildren's hands as new "leaves."

On a large sheet of butcher paper, draw a 46x69-inch rectangle to represent the top of the coverlet. Mark the rectangle into six 23-inch squares. Sketch in the tree and branches (as illustrated in the sample pattern, above), and plan the positions for hands, adding hearts and leaves to fill in the blank areas. This will be your master pattern.

The six 25-inch muslin squares correspond to the squares on the master pattern. They will be joined with 1-inch seam allowances.

Working block by block, cut tree and branch pattern pieces from red polka-dot fabric, adding ½-inch seam allowances to all of the pieces. Fold under seam allowances and stitch tree appliqués to muslin squares.

The squares are now ready for handprints. To make the handprints, refer to the instructions for the handprinted apron on page 126. To minimize mess, plan the printing session for a time when all of your family members are gathered together.

To finish squares, cut out red and maroon hearts, leaves, and simple flower or berry shapes to fill in bare areas of the tree. Stitch these elements in place when all handprints have been completed. With a soft pencil or water-soluble embroidery marker, write in names to correspond to each handprint. Embroider these in stem stitches, using three strands of red embroidery floss.

When the printing, appliqué, and embroidery have been completed, quilt each square block by block. Baste a handprinted square atop a square of batting. Using simple running stitches and white thread, quilt around each of the handprints and appliquéd shapes. Then stitch in parallel rows, approximately ¾ inch from the previously stitched lines. Continue stitching until the entire block is quilted.

To assemble the quilt top, stitch together the three left-hand quilt blocks using 1-inch seam allowances. As the blocks are joined, make sure the outlines of the tree trunk align from block to block. Repeat for the right side, then join the two halves together.

Cut a large red heart from polka-dot fabric. Pin and stitch the heart in place at the top of the tree.

Pin the pieced red lining fabric to the back of the quilt top, and baste it securely in place. Then quilt by hand along the seams and tree branches. Trim off the excess fabric before attaching red bias tape along sides and bottom. Add lace eyelet trim. Finished size of the tree section is 46x69 inches.

To add borders, cut two 86x30-inch side pieces, one 22x48-inch bottom piece, and one 12x48-inch top piece. Fold each border strip in half lengthwise; press. Using a 1-inch seam allowance, attach one raw edge of the bottom border to bottom of the appliquéd coverlet top by laying it under the lace trim and stitching along the lace trim stitching line. Turn coverlet over, press under raw edge, and hem.

Repeat for top border piece. Then add side borders. Finish all raw edges by hand.

Note: If you mail fabric squares and other materials and instructions to those relatives who live too far away to participate in a family hand-printing session, be sure to mark the positions of the hand-prints carefully, so that the resulting piece will fit the overall design of the family tree.

Leaf Pattern Projects

Super simple leaf projects like these are naturals for your kids—and the raw materials are free for the picking!

Leaf Lotto

HOW TO

Materials
Six different kinds of leaves (or more) for each game board
Lightweight white paper (newsprint, typing paper)
Crayons
Colored construction paper and cardboard
Rubber cement

Instructions
For each different type of leaf, make a matching pair of rubbings. Lay the leaf vein-side-up and cover with a sheet of paper. Anchor paper and leaf with one hand and with the other hand, gently rub a crayon back and forth across the paper until the leaf image appears.

Carefully cut out each rubbing and glue it onto colored paper. For each playing board, mount one set of six or more different rubbings of leaves on a large sheet of cardboard. The second set of rubbings will be the matching lotto cards.

Framed Leaves

════════ HOW TO ════════

Materials
Old picture frame (any size)
Two pieces of glass cut to fit frame
Selection of pressed and dried fall leaves
Colored plastic tape
Small nails, screw eyes, clear plastic fishing line

Instructions

For best results, choose brightly colored, well shaped, and fairly thin (rather than fleshy) leaves. Slip

leaves between clean sheets of newspaper and press beneath a stack of heavy books. Allow the leaves to dry out for at least a week before framing them.

To frame, first hinge the two pieces of glass together with colored plastic tape. Use a piece of tape to lift up the top piece of glass (to avoid handling sharp edges) and arrange leaves faceup on the bottom piece of glass. Lower the top piece in place and tape all four sides of the "picture" together.

Slip the glass into the frame and secure with small nails. Add screw eyes, and using clear fishing line, hang in a window.

132

continued

For older children, leaf print projects like these are fun-to-make souvenirs of the fall season. One leaf shape or a variety of shapes and sizes may be repeated for an overall pattern. Fresh leaves work just as well as dried ones for printing, and you can often get as many as a dozen repeat images from a single leaf.

Tablecloth

HOW TO

Materials
**Cotton or cotton-blend table-
   cloth (an old cotton sheet
   also works well)**
Fabric paints
Soft paintbrushes, brayer
Newspapers
Selection of leaves

Instructions
Cover your work surface with newspaper. Spread tablecloth out, faceup, ready for printing.

Scatter leaves across the center of the tablecloth to get an idea of the pattern you want to print. The design can be as simple or complex, and as symmetrical or random, as you wish.

It is often possible to get a number of repeat prints from a single leaf. However, you should have a collection of similar leaves on hand so you can maintain a balance of shapes and sizes in the pattern as you print.

Once you have established a basic pattern, you are ready to begin the printing process. Place a leaf, vein-side-up, on a stack of clean newspapers. Paint the leaf with fabric paint, covering the entire leaf. Try not to put the paint on too thick, or the finished print may look smudgy.

When the leaf is completely covered with an even coat of paint, lift it up and carefully lay it, paint side down, on the cloth. Cover the leaf with a single sheet of clean newspaper and gently roll a brayer back and forth over the leaf several times. Be careful not to move the leaf as you print.

Pick up the newspaper and discard it, then carefully pick up the leaf by the stem. Remove the leaf to another piece of clean newspaper and repeat the painting and printing process—or begin with a fresh leaf.

Once you have started printing, do *not* move the tablecloth while the paint is wet. If you have to reposition the cloth for any reason, pick it up carefully; change the newspapers beneath it before laying the cloth down again.

To produce a pleasing pattern, work from the center of the cloth toward the edges. Try to achieve a balance of shapes, sizes, and colors as you work.

When the center of the pattern is dry, print the corners and borders, if desired. Then press the cloth on the wrong side, following the manufacturer's directions to set the fabric paint and make the color permanent.

Leaf Print T-Shirts

═══HOW TO═══

Materials
**Washed, preshrunk, cotton or
cotton-blend T-shirts**
Fabric paints
Soft paintbrushes, brayer

Newspapers
Selection of leaves

Instructions

Spread a T-shirt out flat on several layers of clean newspaper. Slip several sheets of folded newspaper inside the T-shirt so paint will not soak through to the back while you are printing the front.

Print the shirt with a random leaf pattern, following instructions for inking and printing leaves for the tablecloth, left. When paint is dry, remove the newspapers and press the T-shirt on the wrong side with a hot iron to set color.

Paste-Pot Pictures

If you're low on at-home craft supplies, yet high on imagination, then these pastepot-and-paper pictures are just the ticket for you and your family.

All you'll need to create a galleryful of artwork is a rainbow assortment of colored papers, plus a pot of glue and some nimble fingers (scissors are optional). In a single evening, you and your fellow family artists can fill an entire wall with thrifty masterpieces—all originals!

HOW TO

Materials
Large selection of colored papers in various weights and textures (construction paper, origami papers, gift wrap, foils, newspaper, paper lace doilies, wallpapers, etc.)
Rubber cement
Scissors (optional)
Mat boards; frames

Instructions
There are as many ways to design a pastepot picture—or any other craft project—as there are designers. The first step is simply to become aware of the design sources around you.

Borrowing from nature is one of the most exciting ways of developing a design. Cut a melon, an apple, or a tomato in half and study its pattern (see the picture, above right). Look at shells, tree bark, tire tracks in the snow, or wave lines on the beach for interesting shapes and patterns.

A camera reduces three-dimensional nature to two dimensions, and thus makes the designer's job easier. So study snapshots (or drawings and paintings) of objects, as well as the objects themselves, for design ideas. Take a

closeup photograph of a single flower, for example. Study the picture and reduce the image to its simplest outlines, eliminating all the nonessential details, and you'll come up with a bold, graphic pattern that translates beautifully into a torn paper picture.

To begin, experiment with inexpensive papers (such as newsprint), so you can practice working with line and shape without wasting more expensive colored and textured papers. If you don't like your first efforts, throw them away.

Keep cutting and tearing until you're happy with the shapes you've made. Then move the shapes around until you have a composition that pleases you. Take away what you don't need; add more of what you do need. Always give yourself plenty of elbowroom and time to experiment.

Once you're happy with the design, it's time to glue it down to make a permanent picture.

The backing for your pastepot pictures should be firm enough to prevent warping, and lightweight enough to be easily displayed. Heavy card stock, mat board, and hardboard are all good choices. Plain cardboard may warp, since it absorbs moisture.

Glue all shapes to the background with rubber cement (rub away excess cement with your fingertips after it dries). Then mount each picture behind mat board to

give it a finished look. Frame, if desired. (For more on pretty paper pictures, see pages 62-63.)

• **Tissue paper collages:** The principle of tissue paper collage is much the same as for the pastepot pictures shown here. However, the advantage of tissue paper as a collage material is its translucence; overlapping pieces of tissue paper will blend to form new colors and will yield soft shapes, with slightly blurred edges.

Use the same kinds of background materials as you would for any other paper picture, or try a stretched artist's canvas (which will give the collage an interesting, grainy surface).

For an adhesive, choose a water-soluble polymer or acrylic medium, which soaks into the thin tissue paper and gives the collage a glossy, almost paintlike finish. (Both polymer and acrylic adhesives are available at art supply stores.)

To apply a design to the background, first arrange the tissue paper on the ground until you have created a pleasing pattern. Or, work from a basic sketch and tear tissue pieces as you go.

Working one small area at a time, carefully pour adhesive over the area to be worked, spreading the adhesive evenly with an easy-to-clean nylon-bristled brush. Then lay the tissue paper over the glue, working quickly so that the adhesive doesn't dry before you've applied the design. Continue adding glue and paper until the design is complete. Finish with another coat of adhesive to protect the collage.

After a bit of experimentation, you'll find that tissue paper collage is an amazingly versatile technique that can be used effectively for anything from one-of-a-kind greeting cards to decorating paper lampshades!

Paper Party Favors

Imagine creating an exciting and memorable birthday party for your youngster and his or her friends from things you normally throw away! Ordinary milk cartons, transformed with paint, paper, and tape make delightful party favors for your young partygoers.

Re-create our milk carton truck, circus wagon, and baby buggy, at right, or establish a theme for your little one's special day by making several of one design for the party table's centerpiece. Just picture a table topped with brightly colored trucks, a parade of circus wagons filled with goodies and prizes, or a collection of baby buggies complete with adorable dolls.

To complete the mood of the day, style a variety of party hats from ordinary paper bags decorated with bits of brightly colored plastic and metallic paper plumes.

Milk Carton Toys

HOW TO

Materials
½-gallon milk cartons, rinsed and dried
¼-inch-diameter wood dowels
Spray paint in assorted colors
Utility or craft knife
White glue or glue gun
Stapler and staples
Scraps of colored, adhesive-backed plastic
Clear adhesive-backed plastic or vinyl
White paper, paper doilies
Cardboard egg carton
Felt pens, brads
Black electric tape
Wire handle from paint can
Small wooden beads

Instructions
• **For the truck,** use two ½-gallon cartons. Staple or glue the end flaps together on one carton. Lay carton on its side to create the body of the truck. Cut out a 2-inch area across the top of the carton near its flaps (back of truck). On both sides of the truck body cut two ⅜-inch square holes about ½ inch from the front and back of the body for axles.

Cut the second carton in half (vertically) and save the bottom half for the truck cab. From the top half, cut four 2½-inch-diameter circles for wheels. Cut an X-shaped slit in the center of each wheel to slip the wooden dowel through. Spray paint cartons and wheels in the appropriate colors. Several coats are necessary to completely cover the printing on the cartons.

Cut two adhesive-backed plastic rectangles, each 2¼x2¾ inches, for side windows, and two pieces, each 2¾x3 inches, for front and back windows. Draw profiles of the driver on white paper and color with felt pens. Use the photograph as a guide, or create your own character.

Cut out the profiles and place them on side window rectangles; cover with another rectangle of clear adhesive-backed plastic. Repeat for front view of driver.

Remove the protective backing from adhesive-backed plastic windows and position the windows on the cab. Glue cab on top of body in front of cutout area.

Referring to the photograph for ideas, add other details with electric tape or adhesive-backed plastic. Cut out and spray paint two egg carton sections and glue them to front of truck for headlights.

For wheels, cut two wood dowels into 5-inch lengths; sharpen each end in a pencil sharpener. Slide the dowel through holes cut into the bottom of the truck. Push wheels onto the dowels and glue wooden beads to the ends of the dowels to hold the wheels in place.

• **For the circus wagon,** use two ½-gallon milk cartons. Undo top part of one carton and fold flaps in to make a flat end. Glue in place. Cut out one entire side to become the top of the wagon. Cut notches for wooden dowel axles as for the body of truck. On long sides of wagon, cut out strips to create bars.

Use second carton to cut two decorative tops for sides (see photograph) and four 2½-inch-diameter wheels. Glue decorative tops to wagon body. Spray paint body and wheels desired colors. Add decorative details using adhesive-backed plastic. Then add axles and wheels.

• **For the baby buggy body,** follow the directions for the circus wagon body. Pierce a hole along the top back edge of each side of the buggy large enough to insert the ends of the wire paint can handle.

For buggy top, measure up 4¼ inches from the bottom of the second carton and cut this portion off. Using the bottom section, cut away one side completely; this will be the front. On the sides (adjacent to the front) measure out 1 inch from the lower corners in both directions and draw a line between these two points, making a triangle in each corner. Cut off these triangles. Across the back (opposite from the front), cut off a 1-inch strip. Pierce a hole in each of the side flaps in order to hinge the top to the buggy body.

For wheels, cut four 2½-inch-diameter circles from the discarded carton top and cut an X slit in the center of each one. Spray paint

buggy parts and wheels desired colors. Decorate with doily cutouts. Insert wire handle in holes of body.

Position the buggy top onto the body so the back of the top lines up with the back of the body. Punch holes in the body to correspond with holes in the flaps of the buggy top. Attach the top to the body with brads. Add dowel axles and wheels as for the truck.

Paper Party Hats

═══════HOW TO═══════

Materials
Plain brown paper bags
Colored construction paper
Colored adhesive-backed plastic
Gold stars, circles, and other adhesive-backed stickers
Metallic paper
Yarn

Instructions
Gather, cut, fringe, or fold bags in a variety of fun shapes. Add a chin strap from a folded strip of paper bag or a length of yarn.

Decorate bags with construction paper or adhesive-backed plastic cutouts and stickers. For plumes, cut 8x10-inch sheets of metallic paper into ¼-inch strips. Secure in place with adhesive-backed plastic cutouts.

Dolls and Toys

FROM ODDS & ENDS

Simple playthings crafted from plain, sturdy materials are one of the timeless joys of childhood. Children of all ages will delight in the winsome dolls and imaginative toys described on the following pages.

Especially appealing are these tiny dolls-of-all-nations, designed to please a special little girl. For older children, you might take another tack: Give them a goodly supply of fabric scraps, clothespins, and pipe cleaners, and let the kids create their own miniature figures. Both boys and girls will enjoy creating everything from fanciful fashion dolls to figures of monsters and superheroes out of the same basic range of materials.

For complete instructions on creating these clothespin ladies, please turn the page.

Clothespin Toys

Pint-Size Poppets

The diminutive ladies shown on pages 138-139 are wonderful playtime companions. Make their bodies from clothespins, and use snippets of floral fabrics and trims for their costumes.

──HOW TO──

Materials
Clothespins
Pipe cleaners
Scraps of fabric, ribbon, lace, and gathered eyelets
Brown and black acrylic paint
Red, black fine-tip felt pens
White glue; small paintbrush

Instructions

Paint faces as shown in the photograph, and paint tips of clothespins black for shoes. For arms, center pipe cleaner on the body and wrap around below the neck. Glue and clamp until dry.

For pantaloons, cut 3 inches of gathered eyelet. Wrap and glue around body so that "hem" falls just above shoes, with ends between legs. Cut fabric 3x8½

inches for skirt. Hem and add lace; sew back seam. Gather waist and slip over body with seam in back; glue. Cut trim to crisscross over the shoulders and glue into place.

Accessorize with tiny bouquets, cork hats, and the like for detail.

Lovable Lambs

These lambs are easy to make from scraps of wood and clothespins. Create just one or two, or make an entire flock.

──HOW TO──

Materials
⅝-inch-thick wood scraps
Wooden spring-type clothespins
Old-fashioned wooden clothespins (for legs)
White glue; black acrylic paint
Beads for eyes; metal bells
Fleece fabric
Scraps of black felt and yarn

Instructions

Enlarge the patterns, right, transfer them to wood scraps, and cut out the pieces with a jigsaw. Take apart or cut wooden clothespins to form the legs (see photograph). Glue clothespins to both sides of the body pieces (at the Xs on the pattern). Paint black; let dry. Cut sheepskin patterns from fleece; wrap fleece around bodies and glue in place. Add beaded eyes, felt ears, yarn tails, and small metal bells for finishing details.

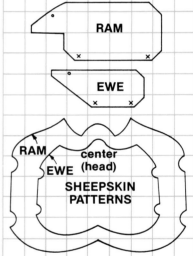

Simple Spoon Dolls

Little ones will love these *whimsical spoon dolls. Make them up in no time using fabric scraps and bits of trim.*

▬▬▬▬ HOW TO ▬▬▬▬

Materials
5- or 6-inch-long wooden spoons
Black, red, and white acrylic paints
Fabric and yarn scraps; trims
Small gold pompons
Fine-tip black felt pen
White glue; white felt
Sandpaper; metallic gold paper

Instructions
Sand spoons. Paint faces on bowl backs with acrylics using full-size patterns, right. Use felt pen for fine lines. Next, enlarge patterns, right; cut out fabric pieces. For sleeves, sew ¼-inch side seams; turn. Turn under raw edge, insert felt hand; sew the hems together, catching the hand in the stitching.

Cut out the dress pieces. Position the sleeves between the dress front and back (right sides together). Stitch sides, catching the sleeve in the seam. Turn. Hem skirt; add lace or rickrack trim.

Turn under neck edge ¼ inch. Gather neckline, insert spoon, and pull gathering thread tightly. Glue neckline to spoon.

To finish, glue trim or pompons to edge of spoon for hat or hair. Add bow or trim. For the choir book, cut folded gold paper to 1¼ x 1½ inches; glue.

1 Square = 1 Inch

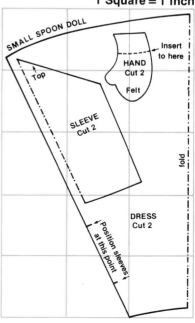

Stitch-and-Stuff Doll Furniture

Cheerful calicos and dainty floral fabrics are perfect for this sweet set of soft furniture. Use your tiniest scraps of lace and trims to fashion old-time antimacassars for chair backs and arms and diminutive throw pillows.

Designed to grace a child's first dollhouse, these stitched and stuffed miniatures are a big hit with adult collectors, too. Make up several extra suites of furniture while you're stitching and set them aside for sure-fire bazaar sales.

HOW TO

Materials
Fabric scraps in small-scale prints, florals, stripes, and solid colors
Scraps of muslin
Fusible webbing
Polyester fiberfill
Small wooden beads (for drawer and door pulls)
Colored pencils or fine-point markers
Embroidery floss
Scraps of lace, ribbon, and trim
Cardboard; scissors

Instructions

Use the table, chairs, chests, and sofa shown here as inspiration for your own furniture designs. After you have mastered the patterns and construction techniques outlined here and on the following pages, you'll be able to develop your own variations on these basic shapes, or design your own.

The general scale of our soft furnishings is approximately 1 foot = 1 inch, and you'll find the pieces appropriate for most playtime dollhouses. The sofa, for example, is approximately 5 inches wide and 2½ inches high. Keep scale in mind as you design your own additional pieces.

• **General construction notes:** Transfer the full-size patterns on pages 144-145 to cardboard and cut out. Trace around the cardboard patterns onto double layers of fabric. You may use different prints for the fronts and backs of the pieces (see sofa and easy chair), or the same print for both (see wing chair).

Add ¼-inch seam allowances to all pieces and cut out. The traced lines will be your stitching guide-

lines. For the sofa and both chairs, be sure to transfer the dotted pattern lines to the fabric as well.

With right sides facing, stitch pieces together, leaving openings for turning. Turn, stuff, and shape each piece, following the specific

notes on construction and shaping that follow below and on the following pages.

• **Easy chair, sofa, and wing chair:** First, cut out and stitch the fronts to the backs as described above. Use ¼-inch seam allowances throughout. Trim seams,

turn the pieces right side out, and press each one carefully.

Next, carefully stuff arm extensions on the sofa and easy chair, and stuff both arms and wing portions on the wing chair. Then sew along dotted lines dividing arms
Continued

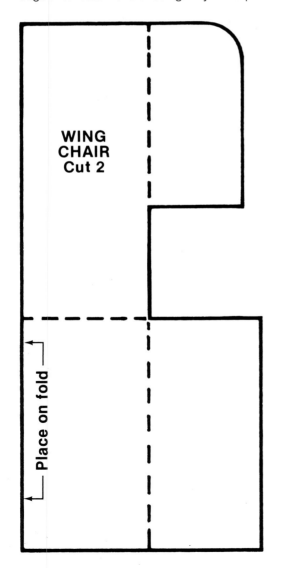

continued

and wings from main portion of chair or sofa.

Stuff backs for all three pieces and, again, sew along dotted lines dividing back from seat of furniture. Finally, stuff seat portion and whipstitch openings closed.

Fold the arms up to meet the back and whipstitch into place. For the wing chair, whipstitch the bottom edges of the wings to the tops of the chair arms.

To make legs for each piece, cut four 1½-inch circles of contrasting or matching fabric. Gather the raw edges of each circle using tiny stitches. Place a small piece of fiberfill inside each circle and gather the edges to make a ball. Stitch one ball foot to each corner of the bottom of the chair or sofa.

• **Coffee table:** First, cut two 2¾-inch-diameter circles for the tabletop and two 1x4¾-inch pieces of contrasting fabric for the base. Stitch the tabletop pieces together. Turn, press, stuff lightly, and slip-stitch the openings.

For the base, sew two strips together, leaving one short end open for turning. Turn, press, stuff, and slip-stitch closed. (Use the eraser end of a pencil if you have difficulty getting stuffing into the tube.) Slip-stitch the two short ends together to make a sort of plump ring. Then stitch base to bottom of tabletop.

• **Dog basket:** Cut two 1x6-inch-long strips for the sides of the basket. With right sides facing, sew the strips together. Turn, press, and lightly stuff. Slip-stitch the end of the tube closed. Sew a line down the middle of the length of the strip.

Cut two 3½x1½-inch ovals for the bottom of the basket. With right sides facing, sew, turn, and press. Stuff the oval lightly, and slip-stitch

WING CHAIR Cut 2

Place on fold

CHINA CUPBOARD Cut 2

closed. Whipstitch the sides of basket in place around the base.

Cut a piece of muslin slightly smaller than the inside of the basket and embroider "Fido" (or the name of your choice) in the center. Tack muslin inside basket.

• **Small chest:** Cut two 3-inch squares for the chest front and back, and two 1½x2¾-inch top pieces. Cut a ½x1¾-inch drawer and two ¾x1¼-inch drawers from contrasting fabric. Fuse drawers in place on front of chest (refer to photograph for positioning). Then topstitch drawer details with contrasting thread.

To assemble chest, sew back to front, then sew ¾-inch mock gussets across each corner.

To make mock gussets, flatten fabric, seam against seam, and sew a ¾-inch-long seam across each corner; seam should fall about ⅜ inch from point of corner. Trim across seam; when turned right side out, the chest will have squared-off corners.

Next, make ¼-inch mock gussets at corners of chest top. Turn, press, and stuff both base and top of chest. Sew openings closed. Tack chest top to bottom; add small beads for drawer pulls.

• **China cupboard:** Cut two rectangular pattern pieces. Cut two ⅞x1⅞-inch cupboard doors from contrasting fabric. Fuse cabinet doors to front of cabinet; topstitch details in contrasting thread.

Following the pattern, cut a rectangle of muslin for the cupboard shelves. Use colored pencils or fine-pointed markers to draw in dishes and shelves. Fuse muslin in place on front of cupboard.

For top cupboard doors, cut four 1¼x2½-inch rectangles of contrasting fabric. With right sides facing, sew two rectangles together; turn, press. Stuff each door lightly and slip-stitch opening. Topstitch around each door, about ⅛ inch from the edges. Set doors aside.

Assemble cupboard, sewing a ¾-inch mock gusset in each corner (see above, under instructions for chest). Slip-stitch doors to the top half of the cupboard, on either side of the china shelves. Add small beads for door pulls.

• **Accessories:** For antimacassars, trim lace to desired size; tack to the backs or arms of furniture.

Use tiny scraps of contrasting fabric or ribbons to make ¾-inch square or round throw pillows. Trim these with narrow bits of lace, if desired.

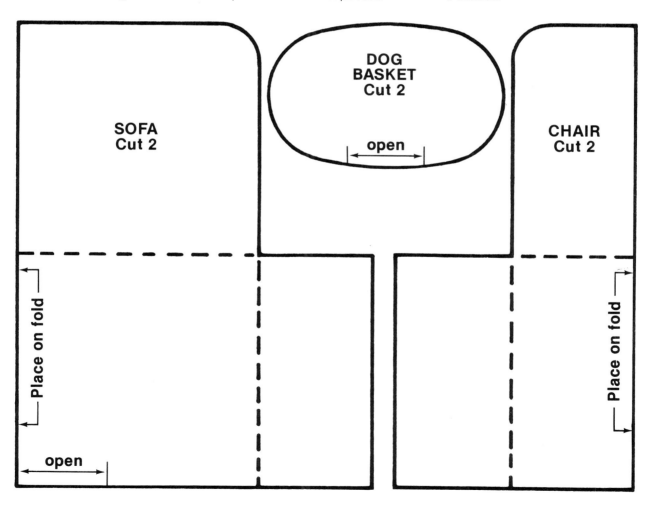

Toy Soldier Dolls

Strike up the band, Toyland-style! You can stitch up an entire brigade of these musically minded toy soldiers from a single Army blanket! And each one makes a wonderful gift for a child or a fanciful collector's item for the young at heart.

The materials list and instructions are for one doll.

HOW TO

Materials
Army blanket or ½ yard medium-weight wool fabric
Scraps of red, flesh-colored, blue, and black felt
10 inches of red nylon upholstery fringe
12 inches each of gold nylon upholstery fringe and narrow gold braid
8 inches of gold cording
22 inches of red middy braid
6 gold beads, 6 black beads
Dressmaker's chalk or pen
Cardboard
Polyester fiberfill
Fabric glue
Black embroidery floss

Instructions
Enlarge the patterns, right, and transfer them to cardboard. Using dressmaker's chalk or a washable needlework pen, trace around the body (flopped, to make a complete pattern) onto a double thickness of blanket or wool fabric. Do not cut out yet.

Open fabric to a single thickness; following pen or chalk lines, stay-stitch around the neck, head, and hat on each piece.

Cut the face from flesh-colored felt; glue it in position atop the stitched outline of the head. (Do this on the side of the fabric *without*

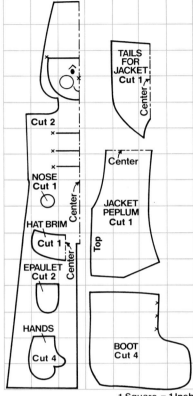

1 Square = 1 Inch

the chalk outline.) Sew the face in place. Embroider the eyebrows and mouth with black thread.

Turn the wool fabric to the side with the chalk outline; sew around the outline, through a double thickness of fabric, leaving one side and leg ends of the doll open. Trim excess fabric, and turn the doll right side out. Owing to the thickness of the fabric, you may find a pair of needlenose pliers helpful for pulling blanket fabric through the opening.

Stuff the doll with fiberfill, beginning with the head and stopping at

the top of the legs. Slip-stitch the side opening closed. Hand-sew across the top of each leg to create a joint.

Stuff the legs through the bottom of the leg openings. Glue a strip of red middy braid over outside seam of each leg to create a red stripe.

Facial features: Cut a ¾-inch circle from flesh-colored felt for the nose. Gather the outside edge, tuck in a small amount of fiberfill, and pull the gathering thread tightly to form a felt bead. Sew the nose to the face. Glue blue felt circles in place for eyes and red felt circles for cheeks.

Boots: On a double thickness of black felt, trace around the boot pattern. Sew along traced lines, leaving the top open. Trim close to the stitching; turn the boot right side out. Stuff the boot to within ½ inch of the top. Slip one leg into the boot, then whipstitch the boot to the leg. Glue a ¾x5½-inch felt strip around the top of the boot to form a cuff. Repeat for the remaining boot. Then, sew three black beads to each boot, along the seam, for buttons.

Jacket and peplum: Cut jacket and tails out of a single thickness of fabric. Sew the tails to the center back of the peplum. Topstitch all around, about ⅛ inch from the edges. Position the peplum at the waist of the doll, overlapping in front, and hand-sew in place. Glue narrow gold trim around the waist along the top edge of the peplum.

Arms: Cut two pieces of wool, each 3⅜x4½ inches. Fold each in half lengthwise and sew ¼-inch side seams; turn right side out. For each hand, trace the hand shape onto a double thickness of flesh-colored felt. Sew around the outline; trim close to stitching (do not turn). Lightly stuff hand.

Slip the hand into one end of the arm and sew across the bottom of the arm, securing the hand in the stitching.

Stuff the arm to the midpoint; stitch across the arm to form the elbow joint. Continue to lightly stuff, stopping ½ inch from the top. Glue red middy trim around the arm, slightly above the hand. Whipstitch the arm to the shoulder edge. Repeat for the second arm.

Collar: Cut a ½x4¾-inch collar from wool. Glue around neck.

Epaulets: For each shoulder, fold 6 inches of gold fringe in half and sew around shoulder, right above arm. Cut epaulets from a single thickness of blanket; glue one on each shoulder. Glue gold braid around edges of each epaulet; trim fringe to desired length.

Glue three strips of gold cording to the jacket front (see photograph). Add six gold beads down the front for buttons.

Hat: Gather 10 inches of red upholstery fringe and tack it to the top of the hat. Cut out the bill of the hat and topstitch around all edges. Hand-sew the bill in a slight curve over the face. For the chin strap, tack the ends of a ¼x5-inch strip of black felt to the outside edges of the bill. Glue a second strip of black felt across the top of the bill.

Tack musical instrument in doll's hand, if desired.

Bandanna Babies

Our sweet-'n'-sassy bandanna babies are quick-to-stitch creations that please doll lovers of all ages.

All you need for one of these adorable dolls are a couple of festive bandannas or pieces of sprightly printed fabric, a dash of fiberfill stuffing, and a touch of whimsy.

Just cut out pieces for the dolls' backs and fronts, stitch together, and gently stuff. For facial features and suggestions of clothing, tack on scraps of felt, laces, trims, or ribbons, buttons, and rickrack details to suit your fancy.

HOW TO

Materials

Two 22-inch square bandannas or pieces of print fabric
Polyester fiberfill
Felt scraps
Ribbon, rickrack, and lace scraps for decorative trimming
Assorted buttons and beads
Fabric glue
Fine-pointed black markers or scraps of black embroidery floss

Instructions

Enlarge the pattern, right, and add ½-inch seam allowances all around. Cut each shape (front and back), carefully positioning the pattern to make the most effective use of the fabric motifs. You can place pattern either horizontally, vertically, or on the bias. Or cut the bandanna in half and stitch the two halves together so that the outside borders meet in the middle of the doll figure, at approximately the waistline. Study the photograph, opposite, for inspiration.

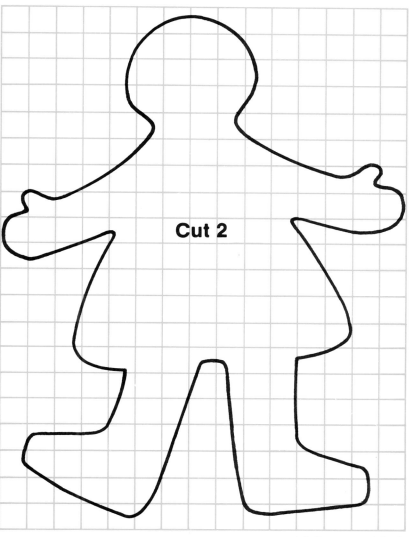

Cut 2

1 Square = 1 Inch

With the right sides of fabric facing, stitch the front and back pieces of each doll together, leaving an opening for turning. Trim the seams, turn the doll right side out, and press carefully. Stuff the doll with fiberfill, and slip-stitch the opening closed.

Use buttons, small felt shapes, simple embroidery (for eyebrows,

for example), and decorative trims to ornament the doll and define her features.

Add bows to insteps, beads to dress fronts, and run rows of rickrack around collars and cuffs. Use a variety of trims imaginatively, but keep embellishments simple to preserve the essentially graphic quality of the doll.

TIPS & TECHNIQUES

Creative Doll Making

Handmade fabric dolls are a delight to make and a joy to give. Whether you're tackling your first rag doll or designing a more sophisticated poppet, the tips below will help you turn out a professional-looking doll every time.

Selecting Materials

For the doll body, choose a firm, closely woven fabric. Unbleached muslin is a practical choice, but you might also consider fabrics that suggest interesting skin textures and colors. Always select the best fabric you can afford, as the body will largely determine the quality of the finished doll.

Select body fabric and yarn for the doll's hair first, then use samples of these materials to coordinate the fabrics and trims for the clothing. Before you begin constructing the doll, lay out all your materials to see that they blend in color, texture, pattern, and scale.

Cutting and Stitching

Lay out your fabric with the right sides together. Then, unless otherwise indicated, position the longest part of the pattern pieces on the lengthwise grain of the fabric.

Instead of cutting out the doll from the fabric before stitching, draw around the patterns on a double thickness of fabric. Stitch directly on the drawn line, leaving openings for turning. Now, cut out 3/8 inch away from the stitching.

Set your machine for 15 to 20 stitches per inch, using the 20-stitch setting when sewing intricate areas such as fingers. Double-stitch all seams using thread that matches your fabric.

Press seams flat on both sides, then press them open. If it's impossible to press the seams with an iron, finger-press instead. Trim seam allowances evenly so the seams will be smooth from the right side; clip curves at even intervals. Clip close to stitching, but never through it.

Stuffing the Doll

Select a filler that is evenly spun, resilient, and free of lumps. Use a pencil eraser, the blunt end of a crochet hook, or wooden chopsticks to assist in stuffing pattern pieces. Avoid objects with points that might pierce the fabric.

Using small quantities of fiberfill at a time, stuff furthermost areas first. Pack fiberfill firmly and stuff all the parts smoothly, checking for lumps on outer surfaces.

Stuffing a doll's hands is often the most difficult step. With a pencil eraser, ease a bit of filler into the hand; use a small, blunt object to move stuffing into one fingertip. Continue until finger is filled; pin across finger to hold in the stuffing. Repeat for each finger, then remove pins and stuff the hand.

To change from moderate stuffing of a hand to firm stuffing of an arm, insert a T-pin through the doll's wrist after stuffing the hand. The pin will form a partial block so the hand won't be too firmly stuffed as fiberfill is pushed into the arm.

Do not stuff arms or legs too firmly at ends where they will join body. Stuff neck areas very firmly to prevent the head from flopping.

Attaching Limbs

For extra durability, use buttonhole twist or pearl cotton to attach arms and legs to the body.

To add interest, you might stitch arms to the body with one arm slightly raised or more forward than the other, rather than having the arms perfectly aligned. Use T-pins, which are longer and stronger than regular pins, to hold arms and legs to the body while determining their positions and while hand-stitching the limbs in place.

To make the hands more realistic, pin a small tuck in the palm of the hands; use tiny blind stitches to secure. On a one-piece hand, you can create the illusion of fingers by hand-stitching the finger lines with matching thread and tiny stitches.

Just for fun, add a dab of powdered rouge to the doll's elbows and knees.

Facial Features

There's no more important part of a doll than its face, for the facial features determine a doll's true personality. Designing the perfect face for your doll takes practice and experimentation, but it will be easier with these guidelines.

To shape the features, first study illustrations, photographs, books about dolls, or dolls you have at home for different types of features. Keep a scrapbook of facial expressions you like, then simplify them to their basic shapes for adaptation to your dolls.

A plastic template of ovals and circles from your crafts store will provide basic shapes that can be used for many facial features. Buy a template with shapes in varying sizes so you can find the shapes that are the right scale for your doll.

Experiment with different features by cutting small pieces of felt into eye and mouth shapes. Cut out and combine several shapes to yield different expressions, then pin pieces to the face to determine proper placement. (See the section on positioning features.)

You can pin tracing paper over the felt pieces and trace them with a pencil, then transfer the outlines to the face for painting or embroidery. Or just appliqué the felt features directly onto the face.

Another way to experiment with facial features is to pencil the face on a piece of muslin, then color the features with crayons. Cut around the face and pin it to the doll's head. Try different combinations of features until you achieve the desired effect. Then transfer the finished pattern to the doll's face for painting or embroidery.

To position the features, use the following hints as a general placement guide.

Eyes: Position the eyes halfway between the chin and the top of the head, leaving a space equal to the width of one eye between them.

Nose: The bottom of the nose should be about halfway between the eyes and the chin, or slightly closer to the chin.

Mouth: Place it halfway between the nose and the chin.

Ears: Position the tops of the ears even with the eyebrows, and the bottoms even with the lower edge of the nose.

For a child's face, the eyes can be rounder and spaced farther apart. Or all of the features can be placed lower on a rounder face.

To apply the features, you can use embroidery, paints, appliqué, or a combination of all three of these techniques.

When painting features on a fabric face, mix a little white glue with acrylic paint to prevent paint from bleeding into the fabric. Use a light touch, small brushes, and practice first on a scrap until you achieve the proper paint consistency.

If you embroider the features, use fewer strands of floss to stitch the small parts, such as nostrils, eyelashes, and eyebrows. On miniature dolls, use regular sewing thread, tiny straight stitches, and French knots for dainty features. Hide the embroidery knots on the doll's scalp where they will be covered by hair.

For appliquéd cheeks, cut circles, hearts, or triangles from red or pink felt or fabric, or embroider cheeks with a circle of running stitches or a smooth circle of satin stitches. For a different effect, try buttons or beads for eyes.

To use inexpensive rouge for cheek color, rub a cotton swab into the rouge cake. Gently blow excess rouge from the ball and lightly rub color on the fabric. Repeat until you achieve the desired effect. Then, to keep the color from rubbing off, spray it *lightly* with hair spray or clear acrylic spray.

Hair

Various yarns, in interesting textures and shades, are ideal for doll hair. Sometimes you can blend two shades or textures of yarn for a special effect, but be careful to keep the size of the yarn strands in scale with the size of the doll.

Use natural fibers such as cotton yarns, linen, twine, untwisted rope and unspun wool as hair for character dolls. For small dolls, use embroidery floss and crewel yarn.

To make yarn curls, wrap acrylic yarn tightly around metal knitting needles. Bake in a 350° oven for five to 10 minutes; let the yarn cool and unwind the curls from the needle. (*Note:* Because the size of the needles determines the looseness of curl, and because some yarns change color as they bake, always test yarn and needles first.)

Make the hair slightly longer than necessary so that the ends can be trimmed evenly later. Then, to attach the hair to the head, "couch" the yarn by sewing over it with matching thread, or use long milliner's needles or large darning needles to stitch a wig to the doll.

Clothing

If you are making your own clothing patterns, use the doll body as a guide for the size. The doll pattern will help determine sleeve and skirt lengths, the width of the bodice, and other measurements. Remember to add enough to the dimensions of the clothing so that you can dress the doll easily.

As you design clothes, cut patterns from paper towels. Towels are soft enough to drape and pleat, and they fold more easily than stiff paper. You can also pin, tape, or baste pieces to visualize the effect of the finished garment.

For your doll's clothing, select fabrics that will not fray or ravel easily. Avoid bulky or flimsy fabrics and fabrics that wrinkle. If you are making an old-fashioned doll, you can give fabrics and laces an antique look by dipping them in a strong solution of hot tea.

Be sure to keep the scale of prints, patterns, trims, and buttons in proportion to the size of the doll. If you find that tiny trims and laces are difficult to pin in place for stitching, spot-glue them in position, then stitch.

For doll stockings, use the tops of infant cotton knit stockings. Turn stocking inside out and slip it on the doll's foot so that top edge of infant stocking is at the place you want top of doll stocking to be.

Pull infant stocking taut to back and bottom of doll foot; pin. Then remove stocking from doll's foot and stitch back and bottom seam following pins. Restitch the seam and trim seam allowance close to stitching. Turn right side out.

To make undergarments, use fine cotton or handkerchief-weight fabric. To reduce bulk, try to eliminate as many seams as possible at the sides and shoulders by combining seam lines with the folds of the fabric.

To make shoes, felt works well. Trace around the doll's foot onto paper for your pattern, then add a ¼-inch seam allowance.

You can make the soles stiff by inserting pieces of cardboard that are cut slightly smaller than the soles. Use iron-on mending tape to add body to shoe pieces, and add miniature straps, buckles, beads, or fringe to embellish the shoes.

A stylish hat can be easily fashioned from a tiny straw basket. Just cut off the handle, turn the basket upside down, and adorn it with flowers and ribbon.

For nearsighted dolls, shape a pair of glasses from florist's wire and then dip them into plastic film, available in craft stores.

Sock Bears and Bunnies

With just a man's sock and bits of fabric and yarn, you can stitch a bunny or bear to delight any young animal lover.

Sock Bears

═══════HOW TO═══════

Materials

Man's heavy ankle-length sock, size 11-11½
1 yard brown yarn
Fiberfill, ribbon, string
Red felt, tapestry needle

Instructions

Lay sock flat. Following dimensions in the first drawing, left, cut off the toe section and top of sock; set aside. In remaining section, cut 4-inch slits along the top and bottom folds of foot to form two flaps.

For legs, turn sock inside out. With right sides together, fold each flap in half (see second drawing, left). Using a ¼-inch seam allowance, stitch as shown. Trim, turn, and stuff firmly to the opening.

Turn under ½ inch along open edge. With double thread, baste along edge, pull tightly to close, stitch to secure. To define head, tie a string tightly around bear's neck.

For arms, lay toe section flat; cut in half up through toe. With right sides facing, leaving top open, stitch from the fold, around the toe, and along the long raw edge, using a ¼-inch seam allowance. Turn arms; stuff firmly. Turn under raw edge, baste opening closed.

For ears, trim ribbed section to 1½ inches wide; cut in half vertically. Stitch, stuff, and close. Stitch arms, ears to body. With yarn, embroider eyes where indicated by dots on third drawing, left. Stitch nose across face, beginning at dot. Embroider mouth; glue a felt tongue in place. Add a ribbon bow.

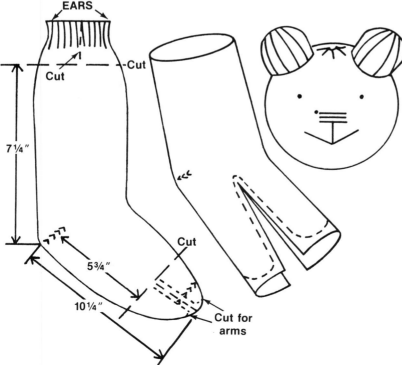

EARS

Cut
Cut
Cut

7¼"

Cut

5¾"

10¼"

Cut for arms

Sock Bunnies

HOW TO

Materials
Man's heavy white sock, size 11-11½
Fabric, felt scraps, ribbon
Pink embroidery floss, black buttons, white pompons
Fiberfill, lightweight wire

Instructions

Cut off enough ribbing to cut two 2x3-inch pieces for legs and two 2½x3½-inch arms for a big bunny (2x2½ inches and 1½x2½ inches for a small bunny). Set aside.

For ears, turn sock inside out, sew narrow V in foot, making sides 7½ inches (large bunny) or 4 inches (baby). Slit sock to point of V. Trim, turn. Insert wire in ear, and tie string at base. Stuff sock so heel forms face. Tie string around neck. Gather bottom closed; stitch.

Embroider face; add button eyes. Sew arms and legs (right sides facing); leave an opening. Turn, stuff, and stitch closed.

Clothing: For jacket, cut two 5½x11-inch rectangles; with right sides facing, sew (¼-inch seams). Turn and close. Cut two 3½x5-inch sleeves; hem long sides, fold in half; sew long edge. Turn, slip over arms, sew to jacket. Fold over jacket top for collar. Add ribbon tie.

Make carrots from felt. Tack legs, pompon tail to body.

For girl, cut 4½x20-inch skirt. Hem one long edge; add lace. Gather opposite edge. Cut two 3½-inch squares for apron. Stitch, adding lace to three sides. Leave fourth edge open. Turn and center apron on gathered skirt edge. Baste. Sew long edge of 4x10-inch bodice to gathered skirt edge. Fold bodice in half lengthwise, hem edges. Attach arms, legs, sleeves, and tail as above.

Wooden Helicopter

Finished size is 6¾ inches high.

HOW TO

Materials
Scraps of 1½-, ¾-, and ¼-inch pine
2-inch-long piece of 1-inch-diameter dowel
4 purchased wooden wheels
Scraps of ¼-inch-diameter dowels
Band saw or jigsaw, drill
Six ⅜-inch wooden buttons
Enamel paints, black marker
Wood glue

Instructions
Enlarge patterns, below right. Cut fuselage and cockpit from 1½-inch stock, cut large rotor from ¾-inch stock, and cut two small tail rotors from ¼-inch stock. Sand all pieces smooth.

Drill ⁵⁄₁₆-inch holes in fuselage to receive ¼-inch-dowel axles for the wheels and rotors. Next, drill ⁵⁄₁₆-inch holes in the top of the 1-inch-diameter dowel piece (the "pilot"), through top of the cockpit, and through bottom of large rotor to receive connecting dowel. Also drill through centers of small rotors.

Paint all pieces in colors of your choice. Draw a simple face on the pilot with the marking pen.

Insert a 2-inch length of dowel through top of cockpit; glue pilot to bottom and rotor to top of dowel. (*Note:* Pilot and rotor assembly should spin freely within cockpit.) Glue cockpit assembly on the fuselage. Insert dowels through holes in fuselage. Add wheels and rotors. Glue painted wood buttons to ends of each axle.

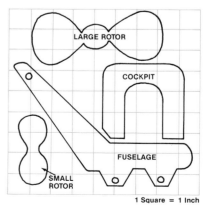

LARGE ROTOR

COCKPIT

FUSELAGE

SMALL ROTOR

1 Square = 1 Inch

Wooden Pull Toy

Finished size is 8¾ inches high.

▬▬▬▬ HOW TO ▬▬▬▬

Materials
Scraps of ¾-inch pine
⅜-inch-diameter dowel (axles);
scrap of 1-inch dowel
Enamel paints, black marker
Nylon cord, wood glue, large
screw hook and eye

Instructions
Enlarge patterns, right. Cut pattern pieces plus eight 2-inch-diameter wheels from pine.

Paint the heads and bodies as shown; draw faces with marker. Clamp matching body pieces together; drill ⁷⁄₁₆-inch holes for axles. Mark and drill head pieces and spacers. Layer and glue together each body section, matching the holes. Clamp; set aside to dry.

Drill a ⅜-inch hole in the center of each wheel. Insert 3¾-inch lengths of dowel through body; glue wheels in place. Knot a 24-inch piece of cord through a ³⁄₁₆-inch hole drilled in neck of one head piece; add knob. Join pieces with hook and eye.

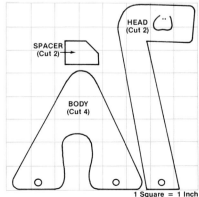

SPACER
(Cut 2)

HEAD
(Cut 2)

BODY
(Cut 4)

1 Square = 1 Inch

Fun for Small Fry

Sponge People

Colorful plastic sponges—the kind that come snugged into packages of a dozen or more at discount stores—are an ideal material for spur-of-the-moment craft projects.

And although our sponge creations won't last through a thorough dunking in the bathtub, they will hold their own through several long, rainy afternoons.

HOW TO

Materials
Plastic sponges in a variety of colors and sizes
Craft glue
Toothpicks and wooden beads to fit on ends of toothpicks
Craft knife or scissors

Instructions
Sketch patterns on paper, using the designs, above, for inspiration. Designs can be either flat figures (like the car and girl), or joined figures (like the little man). Allow sponges to dry before tracing patterns onto sponges and cutting them out with a craft knife.

Cut details from other sponges and glue into place. (The sponge can be cut to half-thickness with a knife when dry.)

For joined figures, or movable parts, insert a toothpick through the layers of the sponge figure. Clip off excess toothpick and glue a tiny bead onto each end.

Soft Blocks

The bright and bouncy alphabet blocks, at right, are safe as well as instructional. Materials list and directions, below, are for six 5-inch square blocks.

═══HOW TO═══

Materials
1 yard of lightweight, natural canvas
Polyester fiberfill
Nontoxic, waterproof markers in assorted bright colors

Instructions
Cut six 6-inch squares from natural canvas for each block. Trace simple letters and motifs from children's books or make up your own designs and transfer them to the canvas squares. Color the designs with nontoxic, waterproof pens.

Before stitching squares together, lay them out to make sure they face in compatible directions. With right sides facing, sew six squares into a cube, using ½-inch seams. Leave two adjacent sides open for turning and stuffing. Turn cube right side out, stuff tightly with fiberfill, and slip-stitch openings.

Wrapping Paper Puzzles

Use spray glue, plywood backing, and a jigsaw to turn any sheet of wrapping paper or a printed poster into a custom-designed puzzle for your child. Kids can even make up puzzles for themselves or their friends, if you substitute sturdy cardboard and school scissors for the more-difficult-to-work-with plywood and jigsaw.

═══HOW TO═══

Materials
Wrapping paper, magazine photos, or poster pictures
Spray adhesive
Plywood or sturdy cardboard
Jigsaw or scissors
Printer's brayer
Clear acrylic spray (optional)

Instructions
Give the back of the paper or picture a heavy, even coat of spray adhesive. Let glue dry slightly (until tacky), then press paper onto plywood. Smooth paper with brayer, to eliminate all air bubbles and create a tight bond. Trim plywood to size, if necessary. Protect the picture with several coats of clear acrylic spray, if desired, then cut the picture into fanciful shapes on your jigsaw.

If children want to make their own puzzles, glue the picture to cardboard rather than plywood, and let them cut out the puzzle shapes with scissors.

Place the completed puzzle on a piece of cardboard cut to size and cover with plastic wrap to hold pieces together when the puzzle is not in use.

Tin Can Toy Train

Have you ever thought about what you could do with those interestingly shaped tin cans that everybody throws away? Here's a charming and imaginative solution: Start collecting all your favorite shaped cans and make a tin can toy train! It will certainly be a favorite for toddler and preschooler alike.

═══HOW TO═══

Materials
Five 3¾-ounce sardine or oyster cans (avoid pull tops if possible)
6½-ounce sardine can
Two 24-tea-bag-size tea tins
8-ounce cocoa tin
6-ounce juice can
7¾-ounce soup can
Cardboard toilet paper tube
20 wooden door pulls for wheels
Wood doweling—diameter to fit hole in door pulls
Black electrician's tape
Spray paint
Adhesive-backed paper
Plastic transfer letters
Spray shellac, paper clips

Epoxy glue or glue gun
Hammer and awl

Instructions
Remove any loose labels and wash cans. *Sand smooth all rough edges to make this toy safe for children's play.*

With a hammer and awl, punch holes in center of each side of large sardine can, and in center of each side of four of the smaller cans. Make holes large enough for the wooden dowel to slide through easily. Punch holes in the center of three sardine cans, on one end of the large sardine can (engine), and on one end of the fourth small sardine can (caboose).

Spray paint the cans the desired colors. Let dry thoroughly. Add details with adhesive-backed paper, plastic transfer letters, and black electrician's tape cut into narrow strips. If transfer letters are used, cans should be sprayed with shellac to prevent them from chipping.

Using a glue gun or epoxy, glue the cocoa can and small soup can to the large sardine can to make the engine (see photograph). For the box car, glue a tea tin to the bottom side of a small sardine can.

The caboose is made from a tea tin glued to the bottom of a sardine can with another sardine can (bottom side up) on top. Glue the juice can to the bottom of a sardine can to create the tanker. The coal car is simply an up-turned sardine can.

Notch the toilet paper tube to fit as the chimney on the engine. Spray paint or cover with adhesive-backed paper; glue in place.

For wheels, spray paint wooden door pulls the desired colors. Cut the wood doweling into 4½-inch pieces, two for each car; sand. Slide dowel through holes on sides of each car; glue door pulls to ends for wheels. If doweling is slightly larger than hole, sharpen or sand ends of dowels until they fit.

Bend paper clips to make hooks for train cars. Shape two hooks like elongated Zs for the coal car. The other two hooks should be bent in such a way as to be a straight wire with both ends facing down. Hook cars together. Secure the hook in place on inside edge of each car with electrician's tape.

For a pull toy, punch a hole in the front part of the engine's sardine can and attach a sturdy piece of string.

Whimsical Wooden Space Station

You can build this fantastic space station for your favorite young commander just by using pieces of leftover plywood. Populate it with intergalactic beings created from ordinary wood finials from the lumberyard, or from legs of old tables and chairs from the junk heap.

You may want your young commander to assist in decorating these whimsical beings from outer space. Let your imaginations fly and create exciting creatures with multiple eyes or legs and unusual space uniforms. Fashion an earthly astronaut, a robot, and amusing and imaginative friendly and not-so-friendly creatures.

====HOW TO====

Materials
Unfinished wooden finials in assorted sizes, chair or table legs, or balusters (available from lumberyards)
Sandpaper, gesso
Acrylic paints in colors of your choice, paintbrushes
Polyurethane varnish or clear acrylic spray
Scraps of ¼-inch-thick plywood
Silver paint

Instructions
Using a saw, trim the ends of the finials, if necessary, so they stand easily. Cut interestingly shaped segments from chair or table legs and balusters for the figures. Bottom edges should be flat, so figures will stand.

Sand all wood surfaces smooth, then paint with gesso diluted with water. When dry, sand smooth using fine sandpaper to prepare the wood for painting.

Apply a base coat of paint in whatever color you, or your child, chooses. When dry, use a pencil to sketch outlines of faces, bodies, and garments onto figures. Using the photograph as a guide, make creative use of the shapes of the wooden figures when designing body parts and clothing.

For example, you may wish to include masks or hoods on the faces; eyes, noses, and ears in unusual shapes; an abundance of arms or legs; and imaginative belts, medals, or other gear that visitors to or from outer space might wear.

Paint designs with acrylics in the colors of your choice. Let dry, and varnish, if desired.

To make a space station, use plywood to build a simple platform in whatever shape your imagination suggests and your scraps allow. Paint it silver and trim it with purple as we did, or finish it with bright colors and trims of your own choosing. Reserve a few pieces of wood to assemble a simple "control panel." Embellish it with a variety of painted shapes to represent a video screen, rocket launcher, and other space-age apparatus.

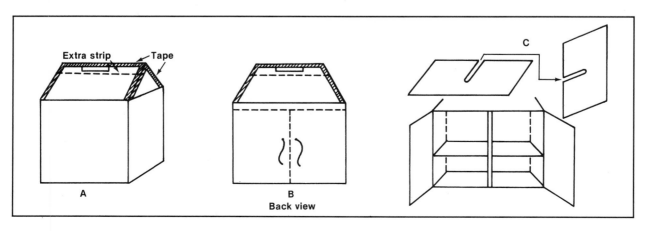

Extra strip   Tape

A

B
Back view

C

Cardboard Dollhouse

A youngster's best-loved toys are often neither fancy, expensive, nor time-consuming to make. For example, in just a few hours, and using the simplest household supplies and materials, you can transform a plain-Jane cardboard carton into an imaginative and portable dollhouse for your child.

So gather up your paints, glue, and scraps of gift wrap and ribbons. In almost no time your favorite little girl will have a lightweight but sturdy new residence for all of her miniature friends.

HOW TO

Materials
Plain corrugated cardboard box
Extra-heavy cardboard for room dividers
Clear acetate for windows
White mat board
Wrapping paper with small-scale designs
Scraps of adhesive-backed paper or plastic
Fabric and lace scraps
Spray paint for house and roof in color of your choice
Acrylic paints
White glue, rubber cement
Double-stick tape
Masking tape
Brown package tape
Craft knife
Permanent, fine-point black felt marking pen
Balsa wood rod (available in hobby shops)
Pencil, ruler

Instructions
Cut end flaps of the cardboard box to form a peak for the roof. If the box does not have them already, cut hand grips in each of the two side flaps (see diagram A, opposite). It may be necessary to add additional cardboard strips to the side flaps to make them extend to

the top of the peak. If so, cut the hand grips in these pieces before taping them to the side flaps.

Using brown package tape for strength, tape the roof together where the side flaps meet the edges of the peak.

Next, spray paint the box the desired color (we used a soft gray paint for the house and flat black for the roof). Several coats may be necessary to cover any printing on the box. Mask off the house portion with newspaper and masking tape before spraying the roof.

With a pencil, mark the outline of the windows on the front and two sides of the house. Cut out windows using a craft knife and ruler.

For the back opening, cut the back side of the box away from the bottom edge and from the top edge 1 inch below the roof (see diagram B). Slit the back of the box down the middle to create two doors. Puncture a small hole in each door, and attach a length of ribbon to each door so doors may be tied closed when your child carries the dollhouse around.

Cut the windows from acetate, making each one slightly larger than the window opening. With double-stick tape, secure windows over the openings from the inside of the house. Draw window panes in place using a permanent felt pen, if desired.

Cut shutters and door from white mat board. Add details with felt

pen. Glue into position with white glue. Cut moldings for the door and windows from mat board; glue. Cut flowerpots and plants from colored adhesive-backed paper and adhere to the windows.

For the room divider, cut one piece of heavy cardboard that is the length times the width of box (for the floors) and a second piece of cardboard the height times the width of the box (for the walls). Cut a slit halfway through in the middle of each piece of cardboard (see diagram C). Insert one piece into the other to create a four-room divider. Set in place and stabilize on each side (under the floor piece) with a scrap of balsa-wood rod glued to the inner wall.

Paper the inside rooms of the box with wrapping paper (or dollhouse wallpaper), and paint or paper the floors. Add rectangular windowsills cut from mat board. Paper and paint the room divider. Make curtains of pleated scraps of fabric, wrapping paper, or paper napkins. Or use bits of lace or paper doilies glued above each of the windows.

Furnish your cardboard house with purchased tables, chairs, and beds. Or, make simple furniture from scrap wood, empty thread spools, jar lids, toothpaste caps, and other commonplace household treasures. Finish with accessories made of wrapping paper or scraps of other paper items. For example, use postcard and greeting card cutouts for wall pictures. Turn the center of a pretty paper plate into a patterned rug. Or, make dresser scarves and fancy bedcovers from paper doilies and napkins.

Use your imagination to create even more great ideas for simple and inexpensive decorations from everyday items. Or, if you prefer, you might like to make several miniature cross-stitch pictures for the walls, or a needlepoint rug or two for the floors.

Pennywise Projects

FOR THE HOME

Nothing beats handicrafts for giving your home personality—and saving you money besides! In this section, we've assembled rugs and lamps, pillows and pictures, and a host of other accessories —all designed to brighten your home without unbalancing the family budget. Included are some helpful hints on how to refurbish and recycle some of the less-than-perfect pieces of furniture you may already have on hand.

Here you'll find practical projects for every room in the house, plus a couple that are just for fun. So why not pick a project, roll up your sleeves, and get started?

You might begin with this thrifty cross-stitched sampler—a graceful illustration of the frugal-but-fanciful approach to decorating that fills these pages. Instructions for this whimsical sampler begin on the next page.

Thrifty Sampler

This colorful cross-stitch sampler is pennywise in word and deed! Use all of the bits and pieces of embroidery floss that you've been saving to stitch this tribute to your thrifty habits—and show off your needlework skills, too.

If counted thread work is new to you, you'll enjoy stitching this sampler, with its simple repeat motifs and completely charted pattern, opposite.

Even if you don't follow the color suggestions to the letter, a "misplaced" shade or two will only add to the charm of this scrap crafter's motto.

HOW TO

Materials
19x21 inches of ecru hardanger cloth or other evenweave fabric
Embroidery floss in a variety of colors, including orange, yellow, and several shades of green
Masking tape
Embroidery hoop
Embroidery needle
Water-erasable pen
Foam-core board, frame
Quilt batting or fleece

Instructions

The finished size of the sampler, including a 1-inch fabric border, is 14½x16¼ inches.

Prepare fabric for stitching by binding the raw edges with masking tape. Then, locate a point in the upper left-hand corner of the fabric 2 inches from the top and 2 inches from the side; mark this point with a water-erasable pen. (This is where you will begin stitching the sampler.)

For best results, mount fabric in an embroidery hoop. Keep it taut at all times while stitching.

Cut 32-inch lengths of embroidery floss, and thread the needle with two strands of orange floss. Use two strands of embroidery floss throughout.

Work the sampler in cross-stitches and running stitches.

To work a cross-stitch, begin by making a stitch that slants from lower left to upper right: Pull the threaded needle through the fabric and count to the right over two threads of the fabric; then count up two threads before inserting the needle into the fabric. Repeat this slanting stitch, always working over two threads, until you reach the end of a row. Then, from the end of the row, work back across the half cross-stitches with a row of stitches that slant from lower right to upper left. This combination will result in an X shape.

Cross-stitches look best if they are uniform in size and if the top, or "crossing," threads lie in the same direction.

To work a running stitch, embroider straight stitches over two threads of the fabric and under two threads; repeat until you reach the end of a row.

Before you begin stitching, thread the needle and knot the tail of the thread. Then, insert the needle into the fabric from the front (top) to the back approximately 3 to 4 inches from the starting point. Do not pull the knot through to the wrong side of the fabric.

Bring the needle up through the fabric at the starting point and work the first series of running stitches.

To finish off the thread, slide the tail of the thread under the previously worked stitches. Finally, snip the knot on the top of the fabric, rethread the needle, and weave this tail under the first row of stitches.

From this point on, begin and end each thread by sliding it under previously worked stitches. Avoid using knots, since they may pull through to the right side of the fabric.

You may choose to start and end threads each time you change colors (as in the flower stems, for example). However, if you decide to work one color until the thread runs out, be sure to carry the thread under previously worked stitches on the wrong side (in the same manner described for starting and ending threads).

To begin stitching, start in the upper left-hand corner of the fabric and work the running stitch border using orange floss. Refer to the diagram, opposite, for placement of stitches and colors.

Stitch the entire border band following the directions on the color key. To avoid unnecessary stitching, be sure to double-check your thread counts before you begin a new row.

Beginning in the upper left-hand corner with the letter U, outline the saying using brown floss. When all of the letters are outlined and completed, fill in the capital letters randomly (in a patchwork manner) using cross-stitches. Vary shapes and colors of each "patch" as often as you like.

Block the finished piece by pressing the fabric on the wrong side using a moderately hot iron and a clean, damp cloth.

To frame the sampler, measure the finished piece and add 1 inch to each side for a fabric border. Cut a piece of foam-core board and batting (or fleece) to this measurement.

Tape batting to the foam-core board. Center the stitchery over the board, taping the excess fabric to the back. Frame as desired.

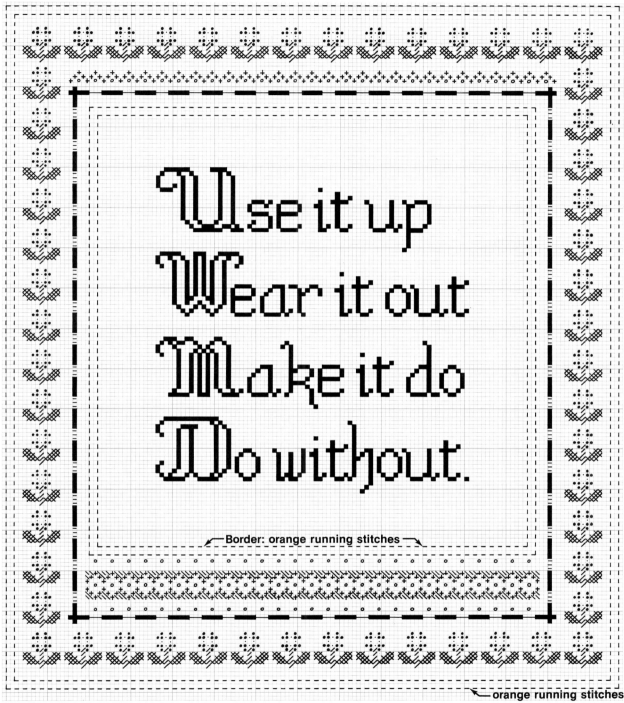

Border: orange running stitches

orange running stitches

1 Square = 1 Cross-stitch
over 2 threads

COLOR KEY
⊡ Yellow flower centers with an occasional red center.
◣ Every other 4-stitch group is coral; otherwise mix colors.
▧ Shade of green.
⊠ Shade of green other than shade used for ▧.
⊟ Variety; change colors as often as desired.
◉ Flower petal colors.   ■ Brown.   ◙ Gold.   ⊞ Dark blue.

Classy Patches

Cut-and-pieced patchwork is the time-honored technique for turning discarded fabric scraps into new whole cloth. Whether you blend a potpourri of remnants into a sprightly crazy-quilt pattern, or choose to work with a more restricted scheme of colors and fabrics, you will find that almost any scrap can be successfully patched into one pattern or another.

Pieced Upholstery

This crazy-quilt will spruce up furniture that needs a special touch.

---HOW TO---

Instructions

To begin, measure the area that is to be covered. Then, cut and piece your fabric swatches into squares; piece these, in turn, into an overall "fabric." Stitch seams and press flat. Embellish seams with featherstitching and add other touches of embroidery for a fancy, Victorian look.

Upholster the piece of furniture as you would with any other fabric.

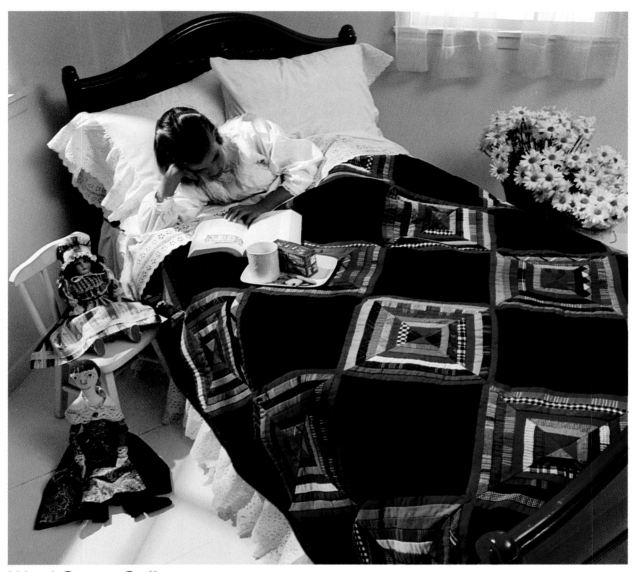

Wool Scrap Quilt

Most patchwork quilts are pieced from lightweight cottons, but soft wool scraps make even cozier coverlets. For the quilt shown above, we used wool scraps for multicolored portions of the design, then invested in several yards of black and red fabric to tie the pattern together.

Instructions below are for a 72-inch-square spread.

===================HOW TO===================

Materials
3 yards black and 1 yard red wool or wool-blend fabric
Assorted wool-blend checks, stripes, plaids, and solids

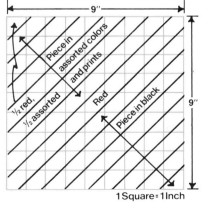

Piece in assorted colors and prints
½ red.
½ assorted
Red
Piece in black
9″
9″
1 Square = 1 Inch

equal to approximately 3 yards
4½ yards of flannel for backing
Lightweight quilt batting

Instructions

Enlarge pattern for one square, left. Cut fabric into 1½-inch-wide strips and piece together, following pattern. Working from upper left to lower right of each square, piece one half of the square in colors and prints. Add a red center strip, then piece remaining half in black strips. Make 64 blocks.

To assemble the quilt top, sew the blocks together into eight rows of eight blocks each. Arrange squares so that multicolored halves meet to form diamond patterns as shown above.

Cut and piece backing fabric to fit. Sandwich batting between backing and quilt top; pin, baste, and quilt by hand or machine. Bind with bias strips of wool.

continued

Log Cabin Tabletop

If your picnic table has seen better days, perk it up with this pretty, cut-and-paste treatment.

For an easy-care, wipe-clean surface, collect odds and ends of self-adhesive plastic paper in complementary colors and patterns (you'll need no more than a yard or two of any one piece). Then plot out your pattern and start snipping!

Instructions below are for a simple log cabin pattern on a square table. Experiment with other geometric patterns and/or shapes to suit the size and shape of your own table.

===HOW TO===

Instructions

First, clean the table thoroughly, using a solvent to remove any wax.

Then use a pencil and yardstick to mark the table into quadrants.

Divide the length of the side of each square by 8; the resulting number is the width of each strip. Cut strips of self-adhesive plastic to this width. Then, for each quadrant, cut a red center square that measures twice the width of the pattern strips.

Next, pencil in the basic lines of the pattern on the table. Position the red center squares in each quadrant. Refer to the photograph to see how the strips are butted together.

Change colors and patterns randomly as you work and continue to add strips until squares are filled. Trim edges carefully to match pattern outlines; smooth plastic flat to eliminate bubbles.

Log Cabin Tablecloth

Subtle patterning in light and dark shades of a single color lends drama to this "straight furrow" variation of the log cabin pattern.

We collected a wide range of blues in solids and prints for our 70x80-inch oval tablecloth—then sparked them with a touch of red. You may choose to substitute fabrics in any color that complements your decor—or that abounds in your scrap bag!

===HOW TO===

Materials
Coordinated cotton and cotton blend fabrics in prints and solids
1 yard of solid-color fabric for log-cabin centers
5 yards of 45-inch-wide fabric for backing
Quilting frame or hoop
Quilting needle and thread
Sandpaper or cardboard

Instructions

Enlarge the diagram for one square, opposite left. Add ¼-inch seam allowances to all pattern pieces. Make templates from fine sandpaper for each of the pattern pieces. Label each template with color and piecing codes (letters and numbers).

Preshrink fabric; cut out pieces. Machine-stitch pieces together, following numbered sequence in the pattern, opposite right.

With right sides facing, stitch piece #2 (color A) to the center square (1). Continue to stitch the pieces together in numbered order, in a clockwise direction, to make a 10-inch square. Press all seams away from the center.

Make a total of 56 quilt blocks and arrange them as shown in the

diagram, far right. Stitch the blocks together, making 7 vertical rows of 8 blocks each.

Next, cut and piece the backing fabric. Press seam open and trim edges of backing to match top.

Pin and baste the backing fabric to the quilt top. Quilt the two layers together by hand or machine, starting in the center and working out to the sides.

To make the tablecloth an oval shape, round the four corners by trimming equal amounts of fabric from each corner. Cut and piece 1-inch-wide bias strips to bind the edges of the tablecloth, turning raw edges under.

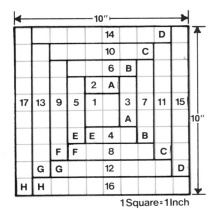

1 Square = 1 Inch

A,B,C,D = light colors
E,F,G,H = dark colors

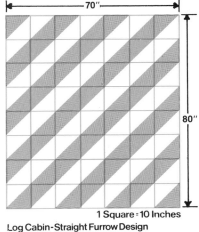

1 Square = 10 Inches

Log Cabin-Straight Furrow Design

Uncommon Artwork

Fabric Still Life

═══ HOW TO ═══

Instructions

To turn a remnant of flowered chintz into a floral collage, starch and press the fabric, then cut out individual blossoms and arrange them on a contrasting fabric background. From a darker scrap of chintz, cut out a simple vase shape as a base for your bouquet.

Glue flowers and vase to background with fabric glue or spray adhesive, working from edges of picture toward center.

Frame picture, then hang it over a table draped with the chintz from which you "picked" your bouquet.

Paper Quilt

═══ HOW TO ═══

Instructions

This dramatic pseudo-stitchery requires no artistic talent—just paper, paste, and patience!

First, outline a quilt pattern of your choice on a sheet of hardboard (we used a quadrant of a quilt pattern for the hanging, above). Next, cut paper pattern pieces for each portion of the design. Then, cut these shapes from patterned gift wrap and glue to the background with rubber cement, working from the center. Protect with clear acrylic spray and frame.

Wood Graphic

═══ HOW TO ═══

Instructions

Make this sophisticated, sunburst graphic from scraps of ¾-inch-thick pine.

First, sketch out a pattern on brown paper. Using a compass draw a bull's-eye segment in the lower right-hand corner. Add a series of five or six evenly spaced lines radiating out to the edges to define the sun's rays.

Cut shapes from ¾-inch lumber; apply stains. Glue pieces to a hardboard and set into a 3-inch-wide scrap pine frame.

Yarn Painting

═══HOW TO═══

Instructions

To re-create this fanciful, folk art hanging, you'll need two 36-inch squares of ¼-inch plywood, a selection of medium-weight yarn scraps and a quart of craft glue.

Cut one piece of plywood into thirty-six 6-inch squares. Sand rough edges. Next draw a simple design or folk art motif onto each square, using the designs, above, as inspiration. Outline each motif with a fine line of glue and press a

strand of yarn in place. Let glue dry, then add glue and yarn to fill in the design. Glue yarn around the border of each square and fill in the space between the motif and border with contrasting yarn.

Assemble squares, and glue to second piece of plywood. Weight squares to avoid warping; dry overnight. Add hooks for hanging.

Low-Cost Lighting

Basket Lamp

Here's a basket lamp with a difference! Coordinate an ordinary basket with a favorite fabric design for sophisticated yet low-cost lighting.

━━━ HOW TO ━━━

Materials
Basket, fabric, and shade
Unfinished lamp base
Light socket
Harp, wire, and plug
Threaded rod, bolts
Acrylic paints in appropriate colors to correspond with your fabric
Small paintbrush
White glue

Instructions

Color the basket with acrylic paints by painting each basket weave a different color. (Or you might try copying a motif from the fabric you've selected.)

To cover the shade, spray it with adhesive and wrap with fabric. Ad-

here seams and excess fabric at edges with white glue.

To assemble lamp, see lamp assembly instructions on page 174.

China Mosaic Lamp

Here's a really smashing way to use your broken, chipped, or cracked pieces of china. Just break the china into small "tiles" and use them to cover an old ginger jar lamp base. Coordinate your china pieces to the colors of a room, as shown above, or use a variety of pieces in different colors and styles for a patchwork effect.

━━━ HOW TO ━━━

Materials
Pieces of cracked, chipped, or broken china
Ginger jar lamp base
Lamp shade
Tile grout
Epoxy

Instructions

Break the china cups, plates, or saucers into small pieces by tapping gently with a hammer. Using epoxy to secure the pieces, arrange them in a pleasing jigsaw fashion on the lamp base. Cover the entire surface, leaving narrow spaces between each piece so the lamp resembles a tile mosaic. Let dry throughly.

Apply white tile grout between the pieces of china to fill all of the spaces. When completely dry, remove excess grout with a soft cloth or sponge.

Rag Lamp Shade

With this simple fabric treatment, you can transform an ordinary wire frame into a unique lampshade with homespun appeal and country flavor! Rip fabric scraps into strips, then wind them around the wire spokes for a lampshade that recalls the charm of the ever-popular rag rug. It's perfect for country

enthusiasts who are looking for something that's extra special.

━━━━━━ HOW TO ━━━━━━

Materials
Metal lampshade frame (pur-chased or salvaged) with an uneven number of spokes or ribs
Fabric scraps or remnants (in assorted prints)
Thread, needle

Instructions
Tear fabric into 2½- to 3-inch-wide strips. Sew strips together, alternating colors, to create several long strips; wrap into balls. Conceal top and bottom hoops of shade by folding a fabric strip in half lengthwise; wrap hoops spirally with the folded fabric strip, placing the folded edge over the raw edge. Stitch the end of the strip to the beginning to secure.

Beginning at the bottom of the shade, wrap one end of a long strip around a rib (spoke); tack in place. Weave strip over and under ribs, wrapping fabric strip around each rib as you work. Join a new strip on the bias when necessary. Continue weaving, crushing down strips to a consistent density. Slip-stitch end to last rib wrapped.

If desired, make tiny stitches between the rows to hold together. Mount on desired lamp base.

Lessons in Lamp Making

Ordinary household items provide unexpected inspiration for attractive, functional, and fun ways to shed some light on the home decorating scene. Even if you've had no more experience working with electricity than flicking a light switch, you'll find that wiring a lamp is nothing to fear.

Most materials for wiring a lamp, including porcelain and metal sockets, wires, switches, plugs, and harps to hold the shade, are available in hardware or lamp supply stores.

Lamp Bases

You can transform almost any object into a lamp or a lamp base, providing it has a passage to receive the cord. Make a hole in the base of the object if necessary, or run the cord through a hollow metal rod. Then, all you need do is add a socket to hold the bulb, a metal harp or other arrangement to hold the shade if necessary, and appropriate wiring.

• A rattan hat stand, for example, makes an inexpensive lamp. (To find a hat stand, check your local variety or display stores.) Just wire a porcelain ceiling socket, screw in a long, skinny showcase bulb, and position the hat stand over the whole thing. (The shape of the showcase bulb prevents contact with the rattan.)

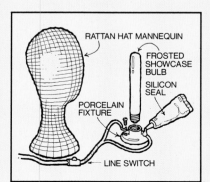

RATTAN HAT MANNEQUIN

FROSTED SHOWCASE BULB

SILICON SEAL

PORCELAIN FIXTURE

LINE SWITCH

Top off the lamp with a straw hat (or any hat of your choice), trimmed with ribbons and posies or simply left "as is".

Be sure to cover the bare wires on the porcelain socket with daubs of silicone rubber sealer (the kind used to caulk the bathtub). Study the diagram, below left, for hints on assembling the lamp.

Once you have the wiring of the porcelain fixture down pat (and have learned to wire an on-off switch and a plug), you can use the same procedures to make a table lamp from almost any item that is translucent enough to let light from a bulb shine through.

• Turn an opaque glass vase or an old ceiling fixture (such as a milk glass globe) upside down over the bulb for a soft, diffused glow of color.

• Place an inexpensive paper lantern over the bulb for an Oriental touch.

• Punch a pattern of holes in a large, clean tin can in imitation of colonial candle lanterns for an attractive display of patterned light. A large nail and a hammer are the only tools needed for this project. For firm backing while punching the holes, fill the can with water and freeze it before you begin. The can will hold its shape while the holes are punched—as long as you work while the ice is still solid.

• Whatever you choose to use for a lamp, remember that the object must be large enough so that the sides of the lamp—whether metal, straw, glass, or fabric—do not touch the bulb.

If you are using a larger (less slender) container for the lamp, you may want to switch to a regular bulb, rather than using a showcase bulb. Or try a clear bulb for an entirely different effect.

In addition, any of the following have interesting possibilities as lamp bases: glass jugs filled with shells or marbles, baskets or metal tins, a child's toy, a piece of driftwood, shapely wooden spindles and chunks of stone masonry, old vases, or candlesticks. The list of adaptable items is nearly endless.

Hanging Lamps

Hanging lamps are easy to make from almost any large, rounded object you might wish to use.

• A beautiful basket makes the perfect shade for a hanging light. If the weave is loose enough, you won't even have to cut a hole in the bottom of the basket for the cord.

Wire the lamp to the ceiling, as shown in the diagram, below. Or hang it through an eye bolt in the ceiling. Run the cord to the corner of the room, down to the baseboard, and along to the nearest outlet. Add a plug and a line switch, and you're all set. Refer to the diagram, below, for the method of assembly.

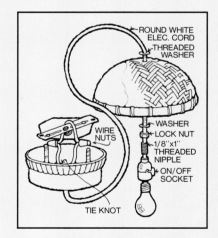

ROUND WHITE ELEC. CORD
THREADED WASHER
WIRE NUTS
WASHER
LOCK NUT
1/8"x1" THREADED NIPPLE
ON/OFF SOCKET
TIE KNOT

• For a high-tech look, use a ⅜-inch-diameter carbon steel bit to drill a hole in the bottom of a stainless steel bowl, a galvanized tin bucket, or a handsome colander.

• Funnels made of glass, plastic, and metal already have the necessary hole to receive the lamp cord—as does a clay flowerpot.

• Or hang an old shade, a shade frame, or a hat-shaped round of cardboard from the wire and drape a square of soft fabric or lace over the frame. For best results, the sides of the fabric square should be neatly finished, and should measure about three times the base width of the shade, allowing for graceful draping and a soft diffusion of the light.

Wiring

The wire used for most lamps is 18-gauge, two-wire rubber- or plastic-covered lamp cord (called 18/2). It is available by the yard and in lamp-making kits at hardware stores and hobby shops. To connect the wire to plugs or sockets, split the insulation at the end of the wire with a knife or razor blade; cut off about ¾ inch of insulation from each wire, as shown below.

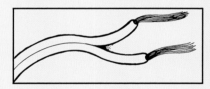

Then unscrew the terminal screws on the plug or socket, and wrap one of the exposed wire ends around each of the screws. Retighten the screws and reassemble the socket or plug.

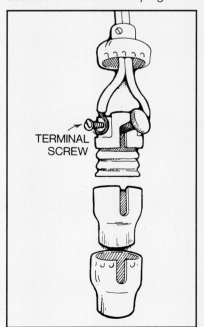

TERMINAL SCREW

To splice lengths of wire, twist the two pairs of wire together, as shown below, and wrap with electrician's tape so that one pair of wires can't touch the other.

TWIST WIRES TOGETHER THEN TAPE

Safety Tips

Always use electrical cord to wire a lamp—or for any home lighting project. Old pieces of wire are liable to be frayed or brittle and may cause shocks or fires.

If you are attaching a lamp wire to a ceiling socket, always turn off the current before making the connection. And never work with lamp cords that are plugged in!

Lampshades

Two of the hanging lamp ideas outlined above also make attractive shades for standing lamps. Select a lacy, bowl-shaped basket to serve as a shade, or drape a pretty scarf or square of fabric over an existing frame for an instant free-form shade.

• Transform an old, straight-sided lamp shade with a fresh coat of fabric. To begin, remove any trim at the top and bottom rims of the shade, then trace a paper pattern to size.

To make a pattern, lay the shade on a large piece of paper, mark a beginning spot, then roll the shade across the paper from the beginning spot all the way around until you hit the same spot again, tracing the edges as you go.

Cut light- to medium-weight fabric to match the pattern, allowing an extra 2 inches on all sides to facilitate fitting the fabric to the shade. Spray the shade lightly with artist's adhesive (the kind that lets you pick up and reposition the work without destroying the effectiveness of the adhesive).

Working from the center front of the shade around the sides and toward the back, press fabric into place. As you work, smooth away all wrinkles with your hands. Overlap seams at the center back about ⅜ inch (match new seam to original one, if there is one). Seal the seam with white glue.

Trim fabric to within ½ inch at the top and bottom edges of the shade; turn excess fabric to inside and glue in place. Add a row of matching or contrasting trim to the edges of the shade, if desired.

• Spruce up a paper or parchment shade with glued-on paper or fabric cutouts. Snip flowers or other motifs from chintz-weight fabric that has been pressed and starched. Arrange the appliqués around the surface of the shade, but try not to overlap the cutouts, because overlapped areas will make unsightly shadows on the shade when the lamp is lit.

When you're pleased with the arrangement, lightly spray the back of each cutout with artist's adhesive. Press it into place, gently smoothing away wrinkles. Make sure that the edges of each appliqué are securely glued down; use white glue to touch up loose spots.

If you decide to use paper cutouts instead of fabric, select designs that are on light- to medium-weight paper and that are printed on one side only. The reverse side of the designs should be either white or a solid, light color; otherwise the printing or pattern on the wrong side will show through when the lamp is lit.

Glue paper cutouts to a shade as described above; protect with clear acrylic spray, if desired.

Finally, remember that you can also purchase metal lamp shade frames from craft and hobby suppliers in a wide range of shapes and sizes—or you can strip the fabric from an old frame and use it as the skeleton for a new shade. These frames can be covered with gathered lengths of fabric, pieced lace patchwork, intricate macrame patterns, or any one of dozens of different craft techniques.

Hooked Alphabet Rug

Hand-hooked rugs make cozy additions to any room—whether traditional or contemporary. A small rug like the one shown below is a handsome way to use up cast-off woolen clothing and fabric scraps that are too small to be incorporated into a braided rug.

Our alphabet rug measures 28x40 inches, but it can easily be sized to your specifications and adapted to a color scheme of your choosing.

To create your own design for a hooked rug, study pictures of old rugs for ideas. Patchwork quilt patterns also provide inspiration about how to combine small amounts of many colors for a stunning visual effect.

Hooked Alphabet Rug

HOW TO

Materials
4-5 lbs. (total) of closely woven wool or wool blend fabrics in assorted colors

32x44 inches of quality burlap for backing
Rug hook and frame (or artist's stretchers and tacks)
Scissors, indelible marker

Instructions

Before you begin, wash all fabrics in warm water to tighten weave and test colorfastness. Then, cutting along straight grain of fabric, cut wool into narrow strips—from ⅛ to ½ inch wide (depending on weight of fabric), and about 12 to 15 inches long.

Enlarge the pattern below to size and transfer to burlap. Draw design from the center of the rug outward, carefully aligning the pattern along the horizontal and vertical threads of the fabric. Go over outlines of the pattern with an indelible marker. Turn under edges of the burlap ½ inch and machine-stitch to prevent raveling.

Stretch the burlap on the frame (or artist's stretchers) and tack in place. Work the pattern one section at a time, and reposition the burlap on the frame as each portion of the rug is completed.

Hook individual design elements first and fill in the background of the rug last. Outline each letter in a single row of beige loops, then fill the letters using blues and pinks or colors of your choice.

Outline the leaves and horizontal and vertical divider "vines" in beige. Fill in leaves in shades of green; hook vines in dark brown. Hook two or three loops of rose, pink, or yellow for each bud.

Finally, fill in background of the alphabet squares with light gray. Hook a 2½-inch-wide border of darker gray around the rug. Fold the remaining, unhooked burlap to the back of the rug, miter corners, and slip-stitch hem in place.

Tips on Rug Hooking

If your rug frame does not have a stand, balance the top edge against a table and the bottom in your lap, so you are working at about a 45-degree angle.

Hold the hook in your right hand, and guide the wool strip along the underside of the burlap with your left hand. (If you are left-handed, reverse the positions.)

To begin, push the tip of the hook through the burlap and pull the tail end of the first strip of wool up to the right side of the burlap.

(All tails will be clipped off flush with the loops of the rug when the hooking is completed.) Put the hook through the next hole in the burlap and pull up a loop of fabric.

You may make loops any height with which you feel comfortable—from ⅛ to ½ inch high—but all loops should be the same height across the entire surface of the work to ensure even wear.

If wool is cut very fine (⅛ inch wide), you will want to pull up loops in almost every mesh of the burlap. If the strips are wider, skip a few threads of burlap between each loop. Loops should be comfortably bunched against each other, but not packed.

When you've finished hooking a strip, bring the tail end up to the surface. Start the next strip by bringing the tail up in the same hole, then continue hooking as before. To begin a new row, skip one or two threads of burlap (depending on the width of the strips) and stagger loops of the new row behind loops of the preceding row.

Clip all fabric tails flush with the surface of the loops; any loops that are too high may also be trimmed, if desired.

1 Square = 2 Inches

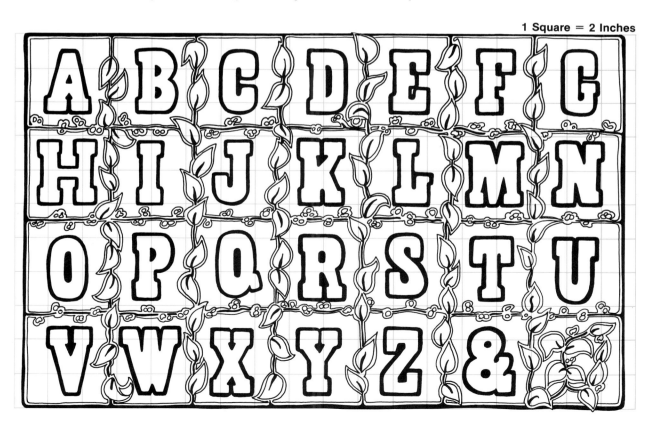

Crocheted Rag Rug and Yo-Yo Quilt

Here are a pair of country-look classics that make clever use of even the most mismatched scraps in your rag bag. Variety is the prime ingredient for success here, and because the pattern is random in both cases, either rug or quilt can be made as large as patience and your supply of scraps allow.

Crocheted Rag Rug

This delightful, multicolored rug proves that there are no hard and fast rules about fabrics for rug making. It's made from an unusual assortment of dress-weight fabrics, including satin, jersey, and faille, which are transformed into a subtly sophisticated blend of colors and patterns when crocheted into this simple rectangular shape.

Our rug is 30x57 inches. To make yours a different size or shape, refer to the how-to instructions on determining the length of the starter strip for the rug.

===== **HOW TO** =====

Materials
**Assorted dress-weight fabrics
and scraps in a variety of colors and prints (you will need
about 9 yards of 44-inch wide
fabrics for a rug with an area
of 10 to 12 square feet)
Size J aluminum crochet hook**

Instructions
First, prepare fabric for cutting. When using old clothing, remove worn spots before cutting. Also remove collars, cuffs, pockets, zippers, and buttons. Open seams and press fabric flat. If you plan to wash your rug (rather than have it dry-cleaned), wash and preshrink all fabrics before cutting them.

Cut or tear fabric into ¾- to 1½-inch-wide strips, depending on the weight of the fabric and on the desired thickness of the rug. Generally, heavy fabrics should be cut narrower than lightweight ones, and all strips from any given fabric should be cut the same width.

Use a yardstick and chalk to mark cutting lines; cut or tear strips on the straight grain to minimize stretching. Sew all strips of any one color or pattern together end to end, joining strips on the bias. Trim seams and press them open.

Fold the raw edges of the fabric strip toward the center, then fold the strips in half to conceal raw edges. Roll these prepared strips into balls and sort fabrics by color and pattern for easy reference.

Starter Strip: To begin making your rug, chain 57 for a starter strip or chain until the starter strip is about 27 inches long. This 27-inch-long strip will form the center of the 30x57-inch rug, opposite. If you wish to make your rectangular rug a different size, determine the length of the starter (center) strip by subtracting the width of your planned rug from its length. For example, for a 3x4-foot rug, the starter strip should be one foot long (4 - 3 = 1).

When crocheting the rug, crochet into the back loops only. (Crochet abbreviations and stitch diagrams are on pages 214-215.)

Rnd 1: Starting with second ch from hook, sc in each loop of the starter chain. At last loop on chain, make a sharp corner by working sc, ch 1, sc, ch 1, sc all in last chain on strip. Work sc in loops of chain back to the starting point. Then sc, ch 1, sc in same loop, sl st to join to last sc, ch 1.

Rnd 2: Sc in each st along the length, (sc, ch 1, sc) in corner ch 1 space, sc in end st(s), (sc, ch 1, sc) in next corner space, sc in each st along the length, (sc, ch 1, sc) in corner ch-1 space, sc in each end st(s), (sc, ch 1, sc) in corner ch-1 space, sl st to ch 1 to join at beg of rnd.

Repeat rnd 2 until rug reaches desired size.

Change colors on the rug whenever you like, or when you come to the end of the strip you're working on. To change colors or add new strips, join a new strip to the preceding one by hand, by stitching the ends of the new strip and the old strip together along the bias. Trim seams, refold edges of strips in toward middle, and continue crocheting.

Treat the completed rug with soil repellent spray, if desired.

• **To make a round rug:** Prepare the fabric strips as above, then work the rug as follows: First make a slipknot and 6 chain stitches in a fabric strip. Join the stitches into a ring with a slip stitch. Crocheting into back loops only, work a single crochet stitch into the first stitch of the ring. Then work another single crochet in the same stitch (an increase). Repeat this procedure in all 6 stitches of the ring.

Thereafter, continue single crocheting, increasing in every other stitch for the second row, and thereafter as often as necessary to maintain the rug's circular shape and flatness.

When the rug is the desired size, trim the last 3 or 4 yards of fabric strips gradually down to about ⅜-inch wide, so that the rug will decrease in width, ending smoothly.

Yo-Yo Quilt

Instructions below are for a double-bed-size throw (approximately 75x87 inches). For a larger or smaller quilt, adjust fabric requirements accordingly.

===== **HOW TO** =====

Materials
**Scraps in assorted colors and
prints equal to 21 yards of
cotton fabric
Sandpaper and pencil
Quilting thread and needle**

Instructions
First make a 3¼-inch circular template from sandpaper. Trace circles on wrong side of fabric and cut out. You should be able to get about 140 circles from one yard of 44/45-inch fabric.

To make yo-yos, turn under raw edges of each circle ⅛ inch and run a line of tiny gathering stitches all the way around the edge. Pull thread to draw edges into center; tie off. Flatten the fabric puff into a 1½-inch circle; press.

Sort completed circles according to color and print. You will need approximately 2,900 yo-yos in order to complete a double-bed-size coverlet—but don't let the number intimidate you! Just stitch up a few yo-yos whenever you have a moment to spare (on the bus, watching TV), and you'll have enough for your quilt before you know it.

To assemble, lay out yo-yos in 50 rows of 58 circles each (or size to suit). Butt edges of circles up against each other and whipstitch yo-yos together.

Cozy Throws

Combine leftover yarns and an adventurous sense of color to create your own versions of these classic afghans.

Knitted Afghan

Finished afghan is 48x58 inches.

═══HOW TO═══

Materials
Approximately 40 ounces of bulky-weight yarn: 2 to 8 ounces each of 10 to 20 colors (2 ounces make 10 rows of pattern)
36-inch-long, size 13 circular knitting needle
Size K aluminum crochet hook

Instructions

Basket-weave pattern is worked over an odd number of sts, as follows: *Row 1:* *Sk one st, sl needle behind skipped st, k the next st and leave it on the needle, k first st, and sl both sts off needle. Rep from * across, ending with k 1.

Row 2: *Sk one st, p second st and leave it on the needle, p first st, sl both sts off the needle. Rep from * across, ending with p 1. Rep Rows 1 and 2 for pat.

Afghan: Cast on 131 sts. Changing colors randomly, work pat st until afghan measures the desired length. Cast off loosely.

Fringe: With one color and size K crochet hook, sc across end of afghan. Next row: ch 4, * sk one sc, dc in next sc, ch 1. Rep from * across. Rep these two rows on other end of afghan. Next, cut four 10-inch lengths of yarn; fold in half and knot through first ch-1 sp on one end of afghan. Using different colors, rep in each ch-1 sp across each end of afghan.

How to Care for Handmade Afghans

Your knitted or crocheted afghan can stay beautiful for years, or look worn in no time—it all depends on how you treat it. Handmade afghans should be given the same care and attention you would lavish on a hand-knitted or hand-crocheted garment.

If you've used wool yarn, expect to wash the afghan by hand. Wash it in the bathtub or a large washtub, so there's sufficient room to swish the afghan about. Use a mild soap and maintain a lukewarm temperature for both washing and rinsing. (To avoid shrinking and fading, don't ever use bleaches or detergents other than those specifically designed for woolens.)

Let the afghan soak, completely submerged, for several minutes, then gently squeeze suds through the fabric. Rinse the afghan thoroughly and gently squeeze out moisture (do *not* wring).

To dry, first roll the afghan in terry cloth towels to remove additional moisture, then spread the afghan flat on clean fresh towels and coax it back into its original shape, squaring up horizontal and vertical edges. Don't hang up the afghan or let it drip dry or dry in direct sunlight or heat.

Wash afghans made of synthetic yarns either by hand or machine. If you wash it in a machine, dry it in a machine, too. Synthetic yarns will stretch when wet and will return to their correct size when dried.

To wash in the machine, use a warmwater setting, a non-bleach detergent, and a gentle cycle. Machine-dry on regular or low heat. To hand-wash, use warm water with any non-bleach detergent. Use cool water for the final rinse. Then dry and block as for woolen afghans.

Crocheted Afghan

Finished afghan is 64x78 inches.

══HOW TO══

Materials
Knitting-worsted weight yarn:
   52 ounces of off-white, plus a
   total of 50 ounces of scrap
   yarn in assorted colors
Size 13 wooden crochet hook,
   or size to obtain gauge given
   below

Gauge: 5 sts = 2 inches.

Instructions

Note: This afghan is worked with two strands of yarn held together throughout—one strand is always off-white.

To begin: With one strand of off-white and one strand of any color, ch 151.

Row 1: Sc in 2nd ch from hook and in each ch across—150 sc; ch 1, turn.

Row 2: Sc in 2nd ch from hook and in each sc across. Rep Row 2 until total length measures 74 inches, or length desired. For a multicolored effect, change the color of the second strand by twisting the colored strands together and holding them under the row until worked.

Border: With a strand of off-white and a strand of color, sc 3 rnds around outside edges of the afghan, working 3 sc in each corner so work lies flat. Fasten off.

Picot edging: Attach 2 strands of off-white along any edge. * Ch 3, sl st at base of ch, sc in next st. Rep from * around, making 3 sts in corner so that work lies flat. Fasten off.

Scrap Yarn Pillows

If your supply of scrap yarn is limited, content yourself with a knitted or crocheted pillow or pillow top worked in either of the two handsome patterns shown here.

Follow the basic pattern instructions but, to begin with, reduce the number of stitches you chain or cast on. For example, to make a 12-inch-square pillow top in the knitted basket-weave pattern opposite, cast on just 33 stitches rather than the full 131 stitches required for the 48-inch-wide afghan. Knit in the basket-weave pattern stitch until the pillow top is the desired length. Cast off, block the knitted square, and back with muslin to preserve its shape. Then back the knitted top with a piece of color-coordinated wool or corduroy. Stuff and stitch closed.

Make similar adjustments to adapt the crochet pattern for any size pillow top you like.

Crafty Catchalls

These clever containers are quick to make using odds and ends of fabric and wood, seashore souvenirs, and leftover wrapping papers.

Coiled Pots

HOW TO

Materials
Plastic flowerpots in assorted shapes and sizes
Medium-size cable cording
Scraps of cotton fabric in assorted prints and solids
Craft glue

Instructions

To make the colorful rounds of fabric-covered cord used to decorate simple plastic flowerpots, begin by tearing cotton fabrics into 1-inch-wide strips. Next, stitch a dozen or so of these strips together, end to end, and use this long strip to cover yards and yards of cording. (Use a zipper foot to stitch cording by machine.)

Line the inside of the pot with fabric, then cover the outside of the pot with craft glue. Let the glue dry until tacky.

Then, working from the top of the pot down, wrap the cording round and round. Glue raw edges of the last coil to the bottom of the pot. Protect it with soil-repellent spray, if desired.

Desk-top Organizer

HOW TO

Materials
Approximately 7 feet of 1x6-inch pine scraps
Wood glue, finishing nails

Instructions

To begin, cut two sizes of 1x6-inch pine—12 inches long for the sides and 4 inches long for the ends and the center divider of the two-space, butt-joined box. Sand pieces, glue box together, and nail to a 24-inch-long 1x6-inch base.

Cut six 6-inch-long dividers and nail to base, adding 1x1-inch spacers between uprights. Varnish.

Seashell Salad Bowl

HOW TO

Materials
Purchased glass or plastic salad bowl
Five or six dozen shells (identical or varied; use shells of your choice)
Clear cement or aquarium sealant

Instructions

First, sort shells according to size and shape. Then, working from the rim of the bowl toward the base, secure shells in place with a good coating of cement or sealant. Place larger shells first, then fill in with smaller shells.

Decoupage Under Glass

HOW TO

Materials
Assorted glass containers
Wrapping papers with interesting motifs
Acrylic gloss medium
White acrylic paint; brushes
Decoupage or nail scissors

Instructions

First clean glass pieces and dry thoroughly. Cut out paper motifs and brush acrylic medium onto the *fronts* of the designs. Affix designs to the inside of the jars and smooth flat. Protect completed designs with several coats of white acrylic paint applied to the inside of the jars with a soft brush.

Kitchen Companions

Here's a batch of budget-minded projects designed to brighten your kitchen.

The heart-bedecked oven mitts can be stitched up in any color combination (to complement your kitchen scheme or a friend's). Cork and clothespin trivets cost next to nothing to make and are hardworking protectors for kitchen work surfaces. There's also a set of clever flatware caddies—great for casual dining and useful for keeping utensils corralled on picnics.

Finally, these projects have an added plus: they're easy to make up in bunches for money-making bazaar sales!

Heart Mitts

━━━━━━HOW TO━━━━━━

Materials
¼ yard each of red and blue cotton or cotton-polyester blend fabric (makes two mitts)
½ yard of calico fabric for lining and appliqués
Thick quilt batting
Red and blue bias tape

Instructions
First, sketch a simple mitten shape by placing your hand on a piece of brown paper and drawing around it. Draw an outline approximately ¾ inch from the actual edge of your hand—then add an additional ½ inch all around for seam allowances.

Cut out two red, two blue, four calico, and four batting shapes. Also cut out four thumb guards, four finger guards, and four hearts from calico fabric.

Appliqué these shapes to the red and blue mitts. Press.

Place batting between appliquéd mitts and calico lining fabric and baste together. Quilt around heart appliqués and along thumb and finger guards, if desired.

Next, with lining sides facing, sew back and front mitt pieces together, leaving bottom open.

Fold bias tape in half and stitch it around the outside edges, and then around the bottom cuff of each mitt.

Cork and Clothespin Trivets

━━━ HOW TO ━━━

Materials
Wooden, spring-type clothespins
Liquid fabric dye
Unwaxed wine corks (available from kitchen supply outlets)
Waterproof cement

Instructions

For the clothespin trivets, begin by removing the springs from the clothespins. Soak the wooden clothespin halves in warm water. Next, prepare the fabric dye according to package directions and immerse the clothespins in the dye bath. Rinse the pins under cool tap water until the water runs clear. Let pieces dry on layers of paper towels or newspaper.

When dry, glue the clothespin halves together to make an 8-inch-diameter circle. (You'll need approximately 28 clothespins for each trivet.) Weight trivets overnight, until glue dries, to prevent warping.

To make the cork trivets, cover work surface with waxed paper or aluminum foil. Glue the corks together either end to end or side by side, using an ample amount of glue. Shape the trivets as desired (squares, circles, triangles, rectangles, etc.), making sure that corks are even across top and bottom. Wipe off excess glue and let dry.

Flatware Caddies

━━━ HOW TO ━━━

Materials
Scraps of solid-color and calico fabrics
Contrasting bias binding
Quilt batting

Instructions

To make a pattern for the caddies, sketch a 3x6-inch rectangle on paper. Round the corners slightly to form an elongated oval shape. Cut two shapes from solid-color fabric, two from calico, and two from batting.

Place batting between one solid and one calico shape; pin and baste together. Quilt the pieces together by hand or machine, stitching along three vertical lines (or in quilting pattern of your choice). Repeat for the second piece. If you are making several caddies, quilt the large pieces of fabric first, then cut out ovals.

Baste the two pieces together, leaving the top open. Stitch bias binding around the edges. Fold the top edge down and tack in place (see photograph). For matching napkins, hem 16-inch squares of calico or solid-color fabric.

188

continued

Why not plan a country breakfast and perk up your party table with this whimsical flock of crocheted chickens nesting in a ring of straw?

These diminutive hens are actually egg cozies shaped to fit right over hard-cooked eggs to keep them warm for your family and guests. Work them up fast with small amounts of knitting worsted and sportweight yarns.

We've arranged our miniature hens in and around a straw wreath embellished with pinecones and an assortment of dried grasses and flowers. To make one like it, collect and dry an assortment of natural materials from the countryside or around your own home. Or, use seed pods, strawflowers, eucalyptus leaves, baby's-breath, bittersweet, and other colorful findings from the florist shop.

Wreath Nest Centerpiece

========**HOW TO**========

Materials
14-inch-diameter straw wreath
  form
Dried baby's-breath
Eucalyptus branches
24 two-inch-long pinecones
1 larger pinecone
Red dried flowers
Glue, T-pins
Spray varnish

Instructions

Select one area on the wreath form to be the focal point. Using garden clippers, cut the top off the large pinecone to form a pinecone flower. Glue one or more pinecone flowers to the focal point area.

Arrange eucalyptus branches and dried flowers around the focal point. Secure with glue. Arrange baby's-breath; glue into place. Glue pinecones in place. Spray wreath with clear varnish.

If desired, add blown-out eggshells to the arrangement. To blow out eggs, puncture a fresh egg at both ends with a large needle. Press your lips against the eggshell and gently blow the contents into a small container.

Crocheted Egg Cozies

Finished size is 4 inches wide, 3½ inches high.

━━━━━HOW TO━━━━━

Materials
Small amounts of knitting worsted-weight and sport-weight yarns in suitable colors
Small amounts of gold and red sport-weight yarn
Black carpet thread
Sizes G and F aluminum crochet hooks, or size to obtain gauge given below
Darning needle
Sewing needle

Gauge: With larger hook, 7 dc = 2 inches

Instructions

Note on materials: Because only very small amounts of several types of yarns are needed for this project, it is ideal for using up scraps. For the basket, use a commercial or hand-spun 2-ply knitting worsted in a light brown color. For the hen's body, use one strand of a textured novelty yarn held together with a coordinating strand of sport-weight yarn.

In either case, any combination of various-textured and colored yarns may be held together and worked as one strand, if you obtain the correct gauge.

Basket: With larger hook and light brown yarn, and beg at lower edge, ch 24. Being careful not to twist ch, sl st in first ch to form ring.

Rnd 1 (right side): Ch 3 (to count as one dc), dc in each of next 23 ch. Join with sl st to top of ch-3—24 dc; ch 3, turn.

Rnd 2: Sk joining, * *holding back on hook the last lp of each dc, make 4 dc in next dc, yo and draw through all 4 lps on hook*— cluster made; dc in next dc. Rep from * around, ending with cluster. Join with sl st to top of ch-3—12 dc and 12 cl; ch 3, turn.

Rnd 3: Sk joining, dc in each dc and cluster around. Join with sl st to top of ch-3—24 dc, counting ch-3 at center back as one dc. Drop basket yarn. Fasten off.

Hen: Rnd 4: Attach hen body yarn(s) by making a sl knot on hook, yo, and insert hook into top of ch-3, yo, and complete a dc in same place. Dc in each dc around. Join with sl st to top of first dc in rnd; ch 1, do not turn.

Joining row: With ch-1 at center back, fold last rnd in half and working through back lps only of each dc (front lps rem free on right side of work to form ridge), join halves tog by working one sc in each of first 9 pairs of adjacent dcs of Rnd 4, one hdc in 10th pair of dc (to form neck), and 2 dc in the 11th pair of dc (to begin head).

Note: When joining the 12th or last pair of dc from Rnd 4, it may be difficult to work through the back lps only; if so, work through either the front lps, both lps, or any top portion of dcs to join.

Join the 12th pair of dc by working 2 dc, yo, and pull up a lp, yo, and pull yarn through 2 lps on hook, drop lp from larger hook and replace on smaller hook. Drop hen body yarn(s).

Attach gold-colored yarn by pulling through last 2 lps on hook. Work 2 dc with gold-colored yarn all in same 12th pair of adjacent dc from Rnd 4. Drop gold-colored yarn and fasten off. (Beak completed.)

Comb: Attach red yarn by making a sl knot on smaller hook, inserting hook into top of middle dc of hen's head (3rd dc from color change for beak), yo, and complete one sc in same place, ch 4, sl st into 4th ch from hook (picot made), * sc in next dc, picot. Rep from * once more—3 picots. Drop red yarn and fasten off.

Wattle: Attach red yarn by making a sl knot on smaller hook, inserting hook into front side lps of last or 12th pair of dc from Row 4 (under beak), yo, and complete one sc in the same place, ch 4, sl st into 4th ch from hook. Drop red yarn and fasten off.

Wings: For left side wing, make a sl knot with body yarn(s) on larger hook, yo, and holding hen sideways with left side up and head facing, insert hook around post of 6th dc from front Rnd 4, yo, and complete a dc in same place, work 3 more dc in same place. Drop yarn(s) and fasten off. For right-side wing, rep as for left side.

Tail feathers: For center feather, using body yarn(s) and the larger hook, ch 6, sc in 2nd ch from hook, hdc in next ch, dc in each of the last 3 ch across. Leaving a 4-inch tail, cut yarn and fasten off.

Side feathers: (make 2) Using body yarn(s) and larger hook, ch 4, sc in 2nd ch from hook, hdc in next ch, dc in last ch. Leaving a 4-inch tail, cut yarn and fasten off. Placing larger tail feather in center (flanked by two side feathers), stitch feathers to back of hen with darning needle and 4-inch yarn ends.

Eyes: Using carpet thread and sewing needle, embroider eyes.

CRAFT YOUR OWN
Christmas Cheer

Though Christmas comes but once a year, Christmas crafting knows no season. Some of the gifts and decorations on the following pages are make-aheads —labors of love that turn humble odds and ends into holiday heirlooms. Others are eleventh-hour wonders guaranteed to provide maximum impact for minimum time and effort!

Why not start a few projects now and avoid the holiday rush? Turn a cache of discarded neckties into patchwork stockings and party pillows like these (directions begin on the next page). Or, compose one-of-a-kind Christmas collages from last year's stock of greeting cards and gift wraps, or stamp wrapping paper with homemade motifs.

Whatever craft project you choose, be sure to involve the entire family—it's a sure way to spread the spirit of Christmas throughout your home and all through the year.

Trims from Neckties

Discarded neckties are a handy source of beautifully patterned fabric scraps—the ideal raw materials for a marvelous array of gifts and trims. Some projects (like the crazy-quilt stocking) are for-Christmas-only creations. Others, like the fancy fan pillows, make striking one-of-a-kind gifts for any occasion.

Crazy Quilt Stocking

═══HOW TO═══

Materials
12 patterned neckties or similar fabric scraps
1 yard of satin backing or lining fabric
¼ yard muslin
⅓ yard quilt batting
2 yards of cording
Pearl cotton embroidery floss

Instructions
Enlarge the stocking diagram, right, and transfer it to brown paper, adding ½-inch seam allowances all around. Cut out the following pattern pieces: 1 muslin, 3 satin (1 for backing and 2 for lining), and 2 batting.

Remove the lining and interlining from the ties and press tie fabric on the wrong side. Next, cut strips of tie fabric to match each of the stripes indicated on the pattern. Also cut out heel and toe sections. Add ½-inch seam allowances to all pieces.

Baste one batting shape to the front (right side) of the muslin piece. Then baste the first tie strip to the top of the stocking, on top of the batting. To add stripes, pin next tie strip along the lower seam of the first strip (right sides together) and stitch it in place using ½-inch

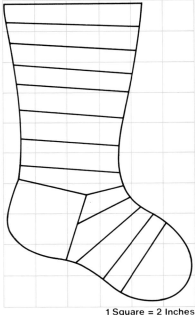

1 Square = 2 Inches

seams. Press this strip toward the bottom of the stocking. Continue pinning, stitching, and pressing the strips until you have completed the toe of the stocking.

Add the heel section last. Fold under raw edges of heel patch and slip-stitch into place.

Use pearl cotton to outline each seam with featherstitching. Cut and piece bias strips of satin lining fabric to cover the cording. Pin and baste covered cording along side and bottom seams of stocking.

Baste the second batting shape to the wrong side of the satin backing piece. Then, with right sides facing, stitch the stocking front and back together. Trim and clip the seams; turn and press the stocking. Hand-sew covered cording around top seam line.

With right sides facing, stitch back and front lining pieces together. Trim and clip seams. Slip lining into the stocking. Turn under the raw edges at the top and whipstitch the lining in place, just below the cording. Add ribbon bow and a loop for hanging.

Fancy Fan Pillows

═══HOW TO═══

Materials
1 yard of black satin or satiny lining fabric for each pillow
Assorted old neckties or similar fabric scraps
1 yard cording
Polyester fiberfill
Quilt batting, embroidery floss (optional)
Compass, brown paper

Instructions
Use the compass to draw a quarter-circle shape on a piece of brown paper (the radius of the circle should be approximately 16 inches).

Next, draw a smaller quarter circle (radius 4 inches) in the corner of the larger arc. Divide the remainder of the circle into seven even, wedge-shaped pieces. Cut each shape from a different scrap of tie silk. Add ¼-inch seam allowances to all pieces.

Turn under raw edges and appliqué spokes and base of the fan to the backing fabric. Baste a square of quilt batting to the back of the appliquéd pillow top and quilt or embroider along seams of the fan pattern, if desired.

Cut and piece bias strips of fabric from satin or printed tie silk to cover cording. Baste cording to front of pillow, along seam line.

With right sides facing, stitch the front and back of the pillow together, leaving an opening for turning. Clip seams, turn pillow, and press. Stuff the pillow with fiberfill and slip-stitch the opening closed.

Gold Doily Wreath

Often, elegance has more to do with ambience and imagination than money. And a mix of unexpected materials can add instant sparkle to any festive occasion.

Press pretty bottles into service as flower vases, sprinkle foil-wrapped candies and tiny gilt packages about for glitter, then top off the display with a glamorous wreath made of gold paper doilies and dried baby's-breath.

HOW TO

Materials
14-inch plastic foam wreath
½ yard of gold lamé fabric
Forty 5-inch-diameter gold foil doilies
Gold spray paint
Baby's-breath or other dried flowers
White adhesive floral clay
Floral picks, straight pins
Wide ecru lace

Instructions

Cut lamé fabric into 1½-inch-wide strips and wrap around wreath. Secure with straight pins.

If backs of paper doilies are white, spray them with gold paint. Set doilies aside to dry.

To assemble doily nosegays, place a wooden pick and a small tuft of baby's-breath on a dab of floral clay. Insert the pick through the center of a gold doily and gather the doily around the flowers. Make 40 such nosegays.

Poke holes in the lamé wrapping on wreath form using an ice pick. Insert a nosegay into each hole, pushing picks deeply into foam.

Trim wreath with a bow made of lamé topped with lace.

Lamé Roses and Satin Ornaments

Lamé Roses

Shiny, quilted roses lend drama to any Christmas centerpiece for just pennies a posy. Mix them with a bouquet of fresh flowers and greens, or tack fabric roses and leaves to a plastic foam base for a luxury-look holiday wreath.

▬HOW TO▬

Materials
**Orange, pink, bronze, and
  green lamé fabric
Dressmaker's carbon paper
Quilt batting
Red, bronze, and green thread
Fabric glue
Green florist wire and tape
12-inch-diameter plastic foam
  wreath**

1 Square=1 Inch

Instructions

Enlarge the patterns, above, to size. Transfer the pattern for the leaves to green lamé, and the pattern for the roses to the remaining colors, using dressmaker's carbon. Do not cut out yet.

Fold lamé in half, with the pattern side up; slip a piece of quilt batting between the fold. Pin the layers together outside the edges of the roses, so that pin marks won't show.

Using straight stitches and thread a shade darker than the lamé fabric, machine-quilt along lines in the roses and leaves, working from the center of the design outward. Stitch the outline of the motifs last. Trim excess fabric and batting close to stitching.

Insert a length of florist wire into the base of each flower and leaf, then wrap stems with florist tape.

Arrange flowers and leaves in a bouquet, along with fresh flowers and greens. Or, for a spectacular holiday wreath, pin and glue roses and leaves to a plastic foam base that has been wrapped in strips of pink lamé. Trim with a suitably sumptuous bow.

Satin Balls

Heirloom baubles are pieced from scraps of satin fabrics and tie silks, then trimmed with gold braid.

=====HOW TO=====

Materials
4-inch plastic foam balls
Scraps of satiny fabrics
Gilt trim and ribbons
Straight pins, white glue

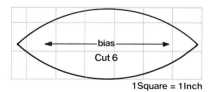

bias
Cut 6

1 Square = 1 Inch

Instructions
Enlarge the pattern, above, and cut six shapes from various elegant fabrics. Be careful to cut all shapes on the bias, as indicated on pattern.

With pins and glue, apply fabric segments to a plastic foam ball, stretching fabric slightly so it lies flat against the ball. Pieces should be evenly distributed around ball; edges should just barely overlap. Trim excess fabric, if necessary.

Cover overlaps between segments with lengths of gold trim; glue into place. Attach bows of gold ribbon to the top of each ball with straight pins and glue; add a large loop for hanging.

Adjust size of pattern for larger or smaller ornaments.

Heirloom Accents for the Holidays

Here are yet more ways to turn treasured scraps into one-of-a-kind Christmas creations. Even a tiny snippet or two of silk and satin, lace or lamé, can evoke the stately elegance of a Victorian holiday.

But if country cozy is more to your taste, transpose the elegant accessories shown above (and on the preceding pages) into down-home trims in a twinkling. All it takes is a simple switch in materials.

For instance, try patching the stocking from woolen scraps in muted shades. Or use humble pearl cotton thread for the lacy casing on the ball ornaments. The designs are adaptable and the choice, as always, is yours!

Necktie Wreath

Just snip the ends off cast-off ties to make the silky "leaves" for this unusual wreath

HOW TO

Materials
14-inch plastic foam wreath
2 to 3 dozen neckties
Scraps of quilt batting
⅓ yard of satin lining fabric
Straight pins, white glue
Ribbon or fabric for bow

Instructions
Wrap wreath form with 3-inch-wide strips of lining fabric; secure with pins dipped in white glue.

For "leaves," cut top and bottom 3½ inches from ends of each tie (set remaining fabric aside for other projects). Remove lining and interlining. Back each shape with a scrap of batting; fold fabric edges under and whipstitch to batting.

Make about 76 leaves. (If necessary, cut extra tie fabric into matching shapes.)

Gather each leaf along straight edge; tie off. Arrange the leaves in an overlapping pattern around the wreath; secure leaves with pins dipped in white glue. Add bow.

Buttons and Bows Stocking

This fanciful stocking is a new-style patchwork, pieced from bright, decorative ribbons, and silk and satin fabric scraps.

HOW TO

Materials
½ yard each of muslin, lining fabric, and batting
⅓ yard of satin backing fabric
Scraps of ribbon, lace, and striped or solid fabrics

Old-fashioned pearl buttons in various shapes and sizes
Purchased appliqués or scraps from embroidered towels, handkerchiefs, or doilies.

Instructions
Enlarge the stocking pattern on page 192 to use as a basic shape for the buttons-and-bows stocking, adding ½-inch seam allowances all around. Cut stocking front and back from muslin, batting, and lining fabric. Also cut one stocking shape from backing fabric.

Using the photograph at left for reference, piece scraps of satin and lengths of ribbon together into a rectangle large enough to accommodate the stocking shape. Cut stocking shape from pieced fabric for front of stocking.

Sandwich batting between the pieced front and muslin shape; baste through all three layers. Quilt along seam lines of pieced front.

Tie small bows out of scraps of ribbon, then tack bows, pearl buttons, and lace appliqués at various points across the stocking.

For back, baste muslin, batting, and backing shapes together. With right sides facing, stitch stocking back to front. Turn; press gently.

Cut and sew lining back to front (right sides together; do not turn). Insert lining into stocking. Turn under raw edges along top; slip-stitch together edges of lining and stocking. Add loop for hanging.

Crocheted Satin Ornaments

A lacy network of lamé thread turns dimestore satin balls into elegant boutique ornaments.

═══HOW TO═══

Materials
2½-inch-diameter satin-covered foam balls
Mangelsen's 2-ply gold lamé thread
Size 6 steel crochet hook

Instructions
Note: The crocheted covering for these ornaments is worked in two pieces; work each piece identically, then follow the assembly instructions below. Crochet abbreviations are on page 214.

To start: Ch 12, sl st to form ring.
Rnd 1: Ch 3, dc in joining; work 2 dc in each ch around; sl st to top of ch-3 at beg of rnd—24 dc.
Rnd 2: Ch 7, * sk 2 dc, dc in next dc, ch 4. Rpt from * around; join last ch-4 with sl st to 3rd ch of ch-7 at beg of rnd—8 ch-4 lps.
Rnd 3: Ch 8, * sc in ch-4 lp, ch 4, tr in dc, ch 4. Rpt from * around, ending with sc in ch-4 lp, ch 4, join to last ch-4 with sl st to 4th ch of ch-8 at beg of rnd.
Rnd 4: Ch 10, * double treble (dtr) in tr, ch 5. Rpt from * around; join last ch-5 with sl st to 5th ch of ch-10 at beg of rnd; fasten off.
To assemble: Position two crocheted halves around the ball, aligning dtr's and ch-5's. Join thread in any ch-5 lp of both halves and work 6 sc over lps of both halves. Join to first sc; fasten off.

Lamé Heart Ornaments

Stitch up a whole treeful of these super-simple trapunto ornaments from scraps of lamé or other festive fabrics.

═══HOW TO═══

Materials
Pink lamé scraps (or fabric of your choice)
Muslin scraps
Polyester fiberfill
Sewing thread to match fabric
Monofilament thread

Instructions
Cut a 3½-inch-high heart from a cardboard scrap to serve as the master pattern. Trace around the pattern on the back of the fabric. Cut out two hearts for each ornament, adding ½-inch seam allowances to each piece.

To make a trapunto heart on the front of each ornament, place a muslin scrap on the wrong side of a fabric heart. Machine-sew a smaller heart shape in the center of the fabric heart. Turn the piece over, cut a slit in the muslin, and stuff the small heart with a bit of fiberfill. Slip-stitch the opening closed, and trim excess muslin.

To finish each ornament, place two hearts—a trapuntoed one and a plain one—right sides together. Sew along seam line, leaving an opening for turning. Trim seams, turn, stuff, and slip-stitch closed. Hang the ornament from a loop of clear monofilament thread.

Portrait Ornaments

Why not start a new tradition? Turn your Christmas tree into a real family tree with a collection of portrait ornaments. Make it a point to include everyone from Great Aunt Emmy to the brand-new baby!

═══HOW TO═══

Materials
Round, oval, and rectangular small plastic picture frames (available at craft and hobby shops)
Family snapshots to fit frames
Spray adhesive
Lightweight cardboard
Decorative papers for backing
Gold cord for hanging

Instructions
Cut a piece of cardboard backing for each frame; trim cardboard with a knife so that it fits snugly inside frame. With spray adhesive, affix a portrait to a suitably sized and shaped cardboard piece; trim excess picture, if necessary.

Insert photograph into frame; cover the exposed cardboard with a scrap of decorative paper. Hang ornaments from the tree with a loop of gold cord or satin ribbon.

Christmas Shadow Boxes

Fanciful old-fashioned shadow boxes like these are the perfect cut-and-paste project to work on during a long winter evening by the fire. And if you are one of those people who treasures even the smallest scraps of Christmas gift wrappings and greeting cards because they are "just too pretty to throw away," then you've already got most of the makings for an array of delightful three-dimensional pictures.

Part of the charm, above, lies in the cheerful mix of styles and materials. Cutouts from holiday magazines, old catalogs, and remnants of fabric, lace, and other trims will add variety and textural interest to your display. Just let your own eclectic cache of odds and ends inspire the perfect Christmas fantasy scene!

HOW TO

Materials
Cigar box, candy box, or other sturdy, shallow container (those above measure 14 inches wide, 10 inches high, and 6 inches deep)

Scraps of cotton, velveteen, and satiny fabrics in prints and solid colors

Scenic Christmas gift wrap and greeting cards

Gold and white lace, buttons, beads, and other paper or fabric trims

Narrow metallic or satin ribbons in assorted colors

White glue, rubber cement

Lightweight cardboard

Decoupage or nail scissors

Instructions
First, select pictures from cards and catalogs or magazines to set the theme for your shadow box. Figures should be in harmonious scale, though not necessarily in the same illustrative style. Cut out all the figures with decoupage or nail scissors, and back them with cardboard, if necessary, to stiffen them.

Glue wrapping paper to the outside of the box, then cover the inside of the box with fabric or paper to make a decorative background for your planned vignette. Build up the scene, working from the back of the box toward the front and adding flat or three-dimensional details as they occur to you.

Glue all the figures in place, then add other miniature touches, to make the box look like an old-fashioned parlor, a winter scene, or whatever your fancy dictates.

Finally, frame your creation by gluing decorative gold and lace trims around the edges of the box.

Recycled Greetings

Customized greetings are another graceful way to recycle Christmas cards and gift wraps from one year to the next. Use both the insides (printed messages) and the outsides (pretty pictures) of old cards. And gather up scraps of wrapping paper, magazine pictures, paper doilies, lace, trims, flat gold braid, stick-on letters, seals, and stars. In fact, you can parlay almost any paper scrap into part of a greeting card!

The samples, above, are sweetly sentimental, but you could just as easily paste up a batch of contemporary cards or traditional scenes of Santa and his sleigh. Use what you have on hand, and you'll find a million new ways to say "Merry Christmas!"

HOW TO

Materials
Medium-weight card stock in white and a variety of colors
Scraps of foil and patterned gift wrap
Old greeting cards, postcards, magazine pictures
Christmasy angels, stars, medallions, letters, and other stick-on seals
White and metallic foil paper doilies
Lace trims
Gold paper braid
Colored construction and origami papers
Decoupage or nail scissors
Spray adhesive, rubber cement
Printer's brayer or rolling pin
Purchased envelopes (optional)

Instructions
Using cards in the photograph for inspiration, shift elements for your card around on a plain sheet of paper until you achieve a pleasing composition. Work with major elements first, then position the smaller elements, such as flowers, angels, stars, and seals.

Cut and fold a piece of card stock large enough to accommodate your design. Cover the card with foil or patterned wrapping paper, using spray adhesive. Press paper onto card with a brayer or rolling pin to eliminate wrinkles; trim paper to match edges of card.

Finally, arrange all of the elements on the card and glue them in place with rubber cement. Weight the cards under heavy books overnight to prevent warping. Make matching envelopes for the cards, if desired, from kraft or other sturdy paper. Or, plan sizes of cards to fit purchased envelopes.

Kids' Printing Workshop

A bustling workshop staffed by pint-size printers can churn out yards of thrifty wraps, dozens of lively ornaments and trims, plus personalized cards and gifts, with elf-like ease. And in the process, the "elves" will have the time of their lives!

Start the assembly line rolling by concocting a batch of simple, seasonal homemade stamps. Just cut the kids' favorite holiday shapes from adhesive-backed foam (from the drugstore) and glue the shapes to blocks of wood. Or twist and loop bits of heavy cotton twine into geometric shapes and attach each to a wood block with glue or small nails.

Then set up shop with a plentiful supply of paper, muslin, and colorful inks and let the kids print up a storm!

HOW TO

Materials
Adhesive-backed foam
Sturdy cotton twine
Scrap wood blocks
White glue, small nails
Poster and fabric paints
Printer's brayers, brushes, pie plates
Assorted paper and card stock
Unbleached muslin
Polyester fiberfill

Instructions

Invite children to make drawings of winter animals such as reindeer, rabbits, and birds whose tracks can be seen in the snow. Or select other shapes, such as stars and Christmas trees.

Using the children's drawings as patterns, cut shapes from adhesive-backed foam. Attach the foam shapes to wood block scraps.

To make string-covered blocks for geometric prints, shape string into designs on blocks and secure with glue or small nails.

To practice printing, put a few spoonfuls of paint on a pie plate. Roll brayer in paint and apply paint to foam or rope printing surface. Paint may also be applied with a brush. Press block onto paper, then lift away; avoid dragging or smearing. Repeat or alternate the prints to make a variety of patterns. Clean brayer, brushes, and plates with water.

• **Wrapping paper:** Apply prints to newsprint, kraft, or shelf paper, using poster paint. Hang just-printed paper from an indoor clothesline to dry. Cut gift tags from colored mat board or card stock and print with stamps.

• **Kid-designed cards:** Let the professionals do the printing here. Take your child's black and white line drawing to a local offset printer (check the Yellow Pages under "Printing") and order copies of the design printed onto card stock. Then have children add color to the printed cards with water-soluble markers.

Note: Check with the printer and Postal Service to determine minimum acceptable quantities and sizes before you begin this project.
Continued

continued

• **Tree trims and package ornaments:** Spread prewashed, unbleached muslin atop a layer of clean newspapers. Then stamp individual prints of animals, stars, Christmas trees—or any designs of a child's choice—onto the muslin (see photographs, right).

Use fabric paints for prints, and space stamped designs about 4 inches apart. Allow paint to dry, then set colors with a hot iron, following manufacturer's directions.

Cut out all prints, leaving a 1½-inch border on all sides. Cut matching backs from plain muslin, and stitch backs to fronts ½ inch from the raw edges. Leave openings for turning. Turn and press; stuff ornaments lightly with fiberfill. Slip-stitch openings closed and add perky rope bows at top of each ornament for hanging.

• **Decorated clothing:** Lay prewashed and preshrunk purchased clothing such as the jumper and coveralls, opposite, on a table or other work surface that has been covered with newspapers. Insert folded sheets of newspaper underneath the areas you intend to print, between the front and back of the garment, to prevent paint from bleeding through.

Print designs on clothing with fabric paint and allow to dry thoroughly. Heat-set the color, following manufacturer's directions.

• **Wooden shoes** (or other wooden items): Apply prints with acrylic paints. Varnish shoes when dry to protect designs.

• **Other projects:** Use the techniques described above and your handcrafted stamps to print pillow fronts, T-shirts, Christmas stockings, paper lunch bags—even quilt squares—for a coverlet (perhaps as an older child's holiday gift to a new baby). More ingenious ideas will come to you and the kids as you proceed with your printing workshop.

Christmas Afghan

If you knit or crochet for your family, you already may have everything you need to make this cheerful Christmas afghan. Just use bright-colored yarns to knit the 55 blocks that make up this 60x72-inch patchwork treasure. Because it is worked in stockinette stitches, even a beginning knitter will find this special afghan easy and quick to make.

HOW TO

Materials

Bernat Berella 4 (4-ply knitting worsted yarn) in 4-ounce skeins in the following amounts and colors: 3 white (A); 2 scarlet (B); 1 skein each in tapestry green (C), honey (D), pale olive (E), walnut (F), baby blue (G), old gold (H), pumpkin (I), baby yellow (J), marine blue (K), willow (L), medium orange (M), caramel (N), and black (O). Or, substitute yarns of comparable weight in the colors of your choice
Size 7 knitting needles, or size to obtain gauge given below
Size H aluminum crochet hook
Yarn needle

Gauge: 5 sts = 1 inch; 6 rows = 1 inch.

Abbreviations: See page 212.

Instructions

The afghan consists of 55 rectangles, either plain or featuring a knitted-in pattern. Knit each of the rectangles in stockinette stitch (k 1 row, p 1 row), following the directions and patterns below and on the next four pages.

To assemble the afghan, join the rectangles into eight blocks, indicated by the solid lines on the placement diagram on page 208. (Blocks are keyed with numbers in circles.) Then join the blocks into

the afghan and trim the edges with a crocheted border.

Refer to the placement diagram for the color and size of each square. When finishing squares, always bind off as if to knit.

To read the placement diagram (page 208), find the letter or number on each rectangle. A capital letter on a rectangle means that it is plain, without a knitted-in pattern. Knit the rectangle in the color corresponding to the capital letter in the materials list, above.

On rectangles with a number followed by a letter, the number refers to one of the patterns (pages 209-211), and the letter refers to the color combination stated in the special instructions below. Background color for each rectangle is also specified below.

The other numbers found on the diagram represent the size (in stitches and rows) of each rectangle. For example, rectangle 6b centered along the top edge reads "60x50." The first number always refers to the number of sts cast on, and the second refers to the number of rows worked. To make this rectangle, cast on 60 sts and work evenly for 50 rows.

When working with two colors of yarn in a row, always twist the new yarn around the strand just worked to prevent any holes. Carry the unused color (or colors) loosely behind work. If the unused color(s) is carried along for more than 5 or 6 sts, bring the color used under the unused color every 5 or 6 sts to prevent loose strands across the back.

When a color is separated by a large number of sts for more than a row or two, use separate strands of that color.

Special instructions for each square:

1: Work background in color A.
2: Work background in color E.
3: Work background in color G.
4: Work background in color G.

5: Work background in color A.
5a: Cast on 20 sts in F. Work 7 rows in st st. Begin chart 5 (page 210), referring only to the holly leaf design marked in black Xs, as follows: P 5 in F; attach E and p 1; p in F to end of row. On next row k 13 in F; k 1 in E; k 6 in F. Continue following chart in this manner until leaf is completed. Work 6 more stockinette rows in F, ending with a p row. Cast off all sts on next row.
5b: Follow instructions for 5a, substituting color O for color F, and color A for color E.
6a: Use A for background and I for figures.
6b: Use J for background and K for figures.
7a: Work background in color G.
7b: Use E for background, color C for L, color I for B, color M for middle flower and centers of other two flowers, and I for center of middle flower.
8a: Work background in color N.
8b: Use J for background; replace B with F.
9a: Use E for the background. Work 10 rows in E. On next row k 16 in E; attach C and k 1; attach L and k 1; k 1 in C; k to end of row in E. Follow the next 5 rows of the chart, using 1 strand each of colors E, C, and L. Be careful to bring the threads of colors C and L around last unused color. At end of row, cut off color C thread, but carry same strand of color L up center of tree.

On next row, k 3 in E; attach first strand of C and k 14; k 1 in L; k 14 in C; attach second strand of E and k 3. *Do not cut off thread C at end of row.*

On next row p 3 in E; attach a second strand of L and follow chart across row. *Do not cut off second strand of L at end of row.* On next row, k 3 in E; attach a second strand of C; follow chart across next 2 rows without cutting off second strand of C.

Continued

210

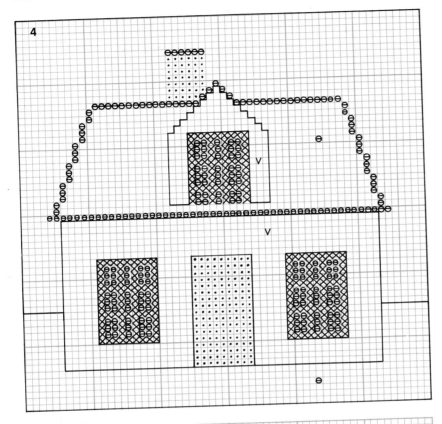

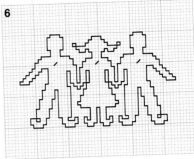

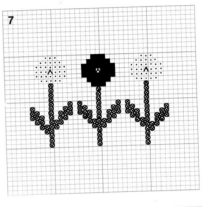

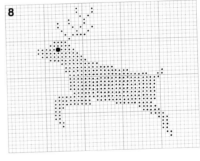

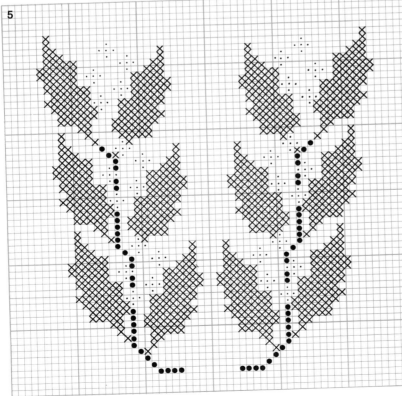

COLOR KEY

- ☐ Background
- ⊖ White
- ⊡ Scarlet
- ☒ Tapestry Green
- Ⅴ Honey
- ⊟ Pale Olive
- ⊞ Walnut
- ⋀ Baby Blue
- ⟍ Old Gold
- ⟋ Pumpkin
- ◯ Baby Yellow
- ■ Marine Blue
- ⊗ Willow
- ◍ Medium Orange
- ⊕ Caramel
- ● Black

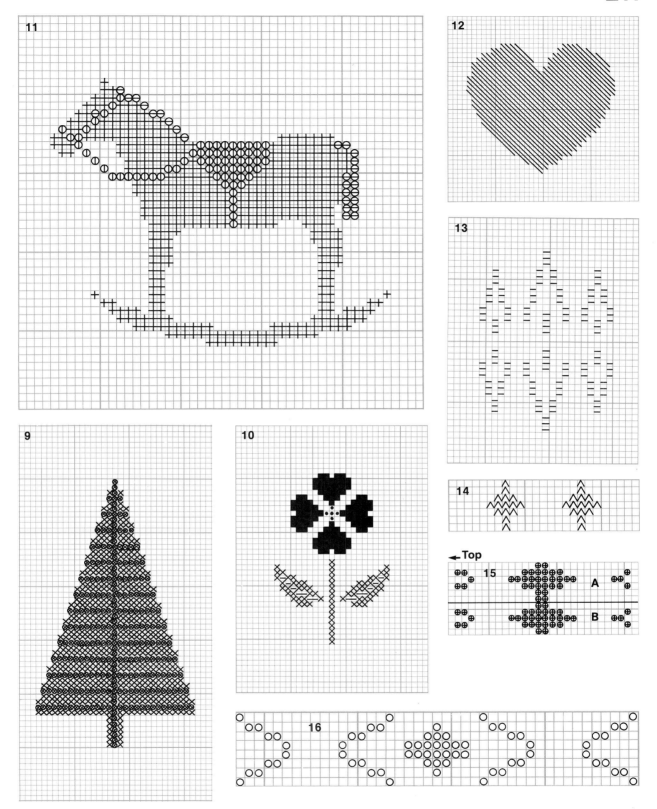

Basic Knitting Stitches

Knitting Abbreviations

beg	beginning
bet	between
dec	decrease
dp	double pointed
inc	increase
k	knit
lp(s)	loops
MC	main color
p	purl
pat	pattern
psso	pass slip stitch over
rem	remaining
rep	repeat
sk	skip
sl st	slip stitch
sp(s)	space(s)
st(s)	stitch(es)
st st	stockinette stitch
tog	together
yo	yarn over
*	repeat whatever follows as indicated.
( )	work directions given in parentheses number of times specified.
work even	continue making pattern as before over same number of stitches without increasing or decreasing.

To cast on, make a slipknot around the needle at a distance from yarn end that equals 1 inch for each stitch to be cast on.

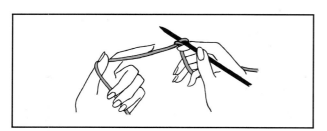

Hold needle that has slipknot in your right hand and make a loop of the short length of yarn around your left thumb.

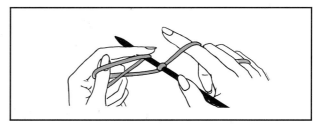

Insert point of needle in your right hand under loop on your left thumb. Loop yarn from ball over fingers of your right hand.

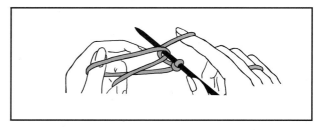

Wind yarn from ball under and over needle and draw it through loop, leaving the stitch on the needle.

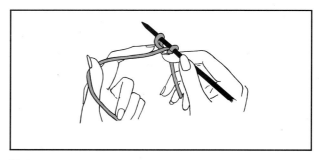

Tighten stitches on needle and bring yarn end around thumb so it is ready for next stitch. Repeat the last four steps until you have the desired number of stitches. Switch needle with stitches to left hand.

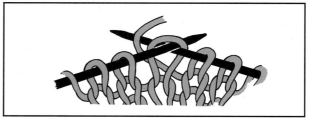

To make a knit stitch, hold needle with stitches in left hand and other needle in right hand. Insert right needle through stitch on left needle from front to back. Pass yarn around point of right needle to form a loop.

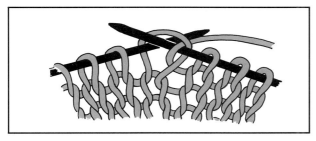

Pull this loop through stitch on left needle and draw loop onto right needle.

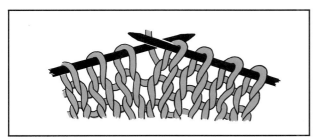

Now slip the stitch completely off of the left needle. Repeat these steps until you have transferred all of the stitches from the left needle to the right needle. This completes one row of knitting. When you begin working on the next row, move the needle holding the stitches to your left hand and the other needle to your right hand.

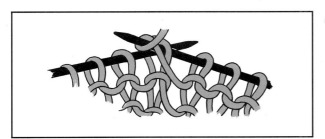

To make a purl stitch, hold the needle with the stitches in your left hand and the other needle in your right hand. Insert the right needle through the stitch on the left needle from back to front. Wind the yarn around the point of right needle to form a loop.

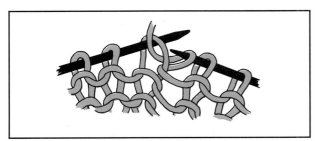

Draw a loop through stitch on the needle in your left hand, and transfer it to the needle in your right hand.

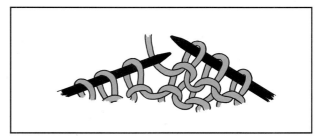

Slip the stitch completely off the left needle. Repeat these steps until all loops on left needle have been transferred to right needle. This completes one row of purling. Switch needles and work next row.

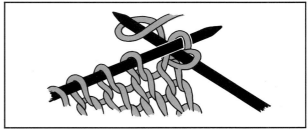

To increase, knit or purl as usual, but do not slip it off the left needle. Instead, insert right needle into back of stitch and knit or purl into the stitch again. Slip both stitches onto right needle, making two stitches. To decrease, knit or purl two stitches together at the same time. To slip a stitch, insert the right needle as if to purl (unless directions read to do it as if to knit). Then slip the stitch onto right needle without working; be careful not to twist stitch.

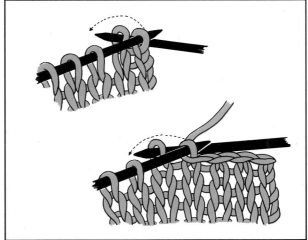

To bind off, work two stitches in pattern loosely. With left needle, lift first stitch over second stitch and off right needle. This binds off one stitch. Repeat this same technique for required number of stitches. To bind off an entire row, continue until one stitch remains, then break the yarn and draw the end through the last stitch.

Basic Crochet Stitches

Crochet Abbreviations

beg	begin(ning)
bet	between
ch	chain
dc	double crochet
dec	decrease
dtr	double treble
hdc	half double crochet
inc	increase
lp(s)	loop(s)
pat	pattern
rep	repeat
rem	remaining
rnd	round
sc	single crochet
sl st	slip stitch
sp(s)	space(s)
st(s)	stitch(es)
tog	together
yo	yarn over
*	repeat whatever follows as indicated.
work even	continue making pattern as before over same number of stitches without increasing or decreasing.

Make the foundation chain by catching strand with hook and drawing it through loop. Make the chain the length called for on the pattern.

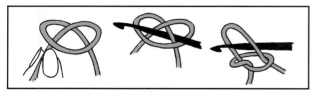

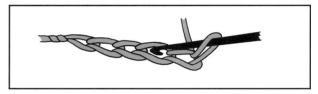

Single crochet: Insert the hook into the second chain from the hook, under two upper strands of yarn.

Start by making a slipknot on the crochet hook about 6 inches from the end of the yarn. Pull one end of the yarn to tighten the knot.

Draw up a loop.

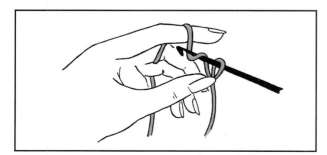

Draw yarn over hook.

Hold the hook between right index finger and thumb, as you would a pencil. Wrap yarn over ring finger, under middle finger and over index finger, holding short end between thumb and index finger. If you need more tension, wrap yarn around little finger. Insert hook under and over strand of yarn.

Pull yarn through the two loops, completing single crochet stitch. Insert hook into next stitch, and repeat last four steps.

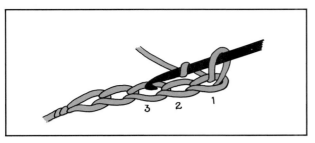

Half double crochet: With yarn over hook, insert hook into third chain, under the two upper strands of yarn.

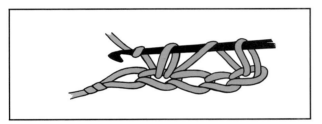

Draw up a loop.

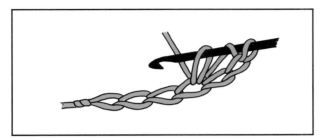

Draw yarn over the hook.

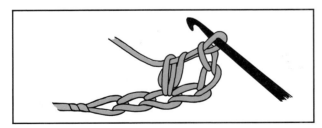

Pull through the three loops, completing the half double crochet.

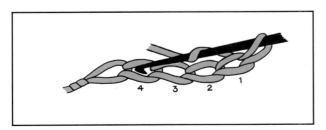

Double crochet: Holding yarn over hook, insert hook into fourth chain, under the two upper strands of yarn.

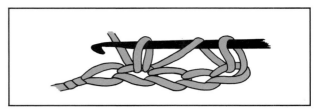

Draw up a loop.

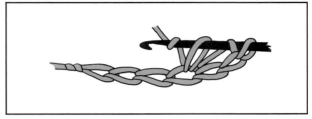

Wrap yarn over hook.

Draw yarn through two loops.

Yarn over again and through last two loops on hook. This completes double crochet.

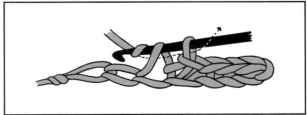

Slip stitch: After you've made the foundation chain, insert the crochet hook under the top strand of the second chain from the hook and yarn over. With a single motion, pull the yarn through the stitch and loop on the hook. Insert the hook under the top strand of the next chain, then yarn over and draw the yarn through the stitch and loop on the hook. Repeat this procedure to the end of the chain.

Basic Embroidery Stitches

Backstitch

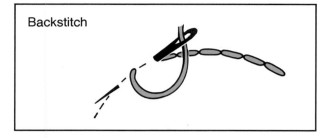

Couching stitch

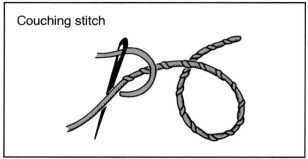

Buttonhole stitch

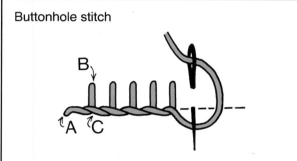

Cross-stitch

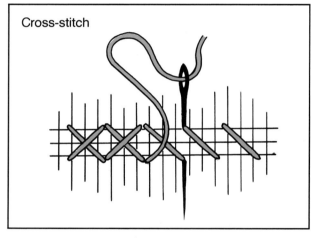

Chain stitch and variations

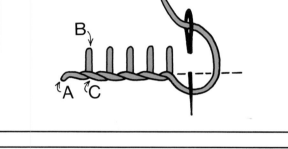

Cable chain stitch

Individual chain stitch

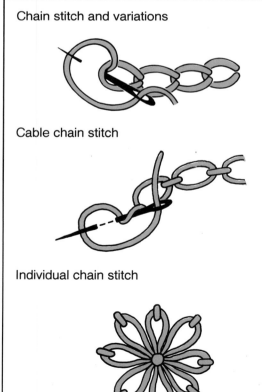

Featherstitch and variations

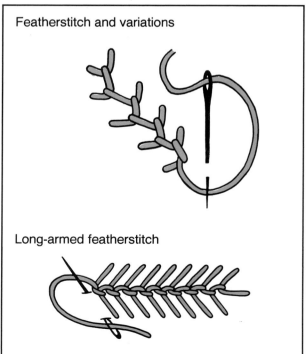

Long-armed featherstitch

French knot

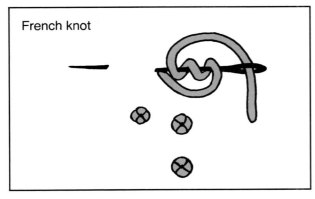

Laid work

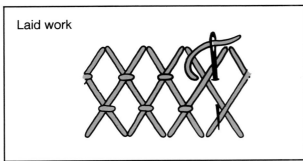

Outline stitch

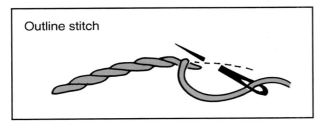

Running stitch

Darning stitch

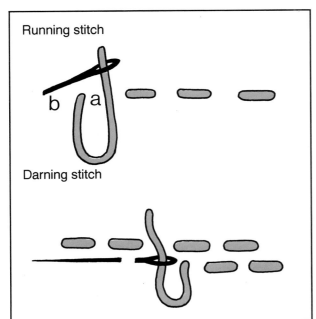

Satin stitch

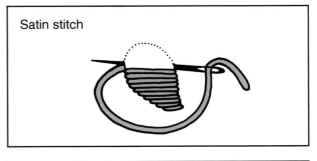

Seed stitch

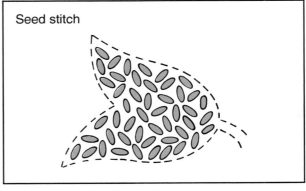

Spiderweb stitch

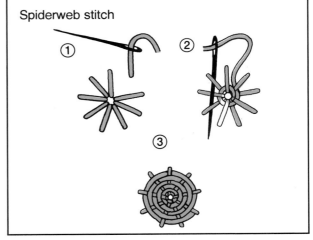

Split stitch

Straight stitch

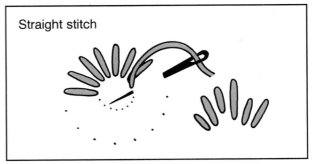

Basic Needlepoint Stitches

Bargello stitch

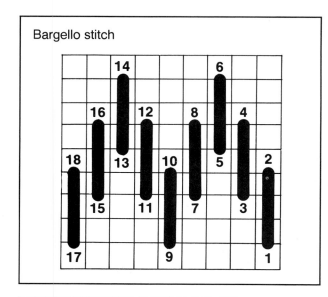

Cross-stitch

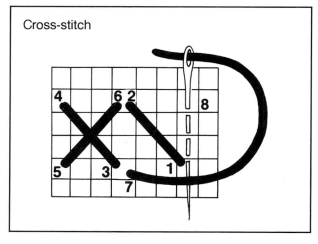

Basket-weave stitch

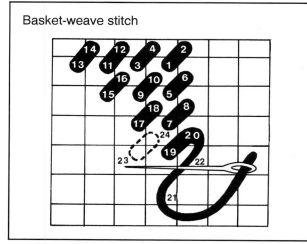

Diamond eyelet stitch

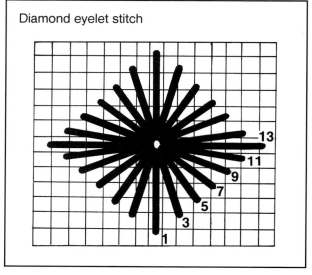

Continental stitch

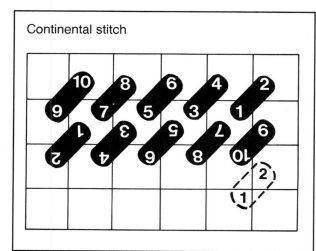

French knot

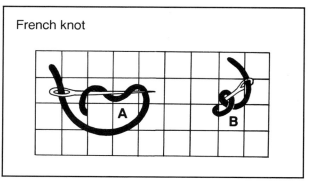

Half cross-stitch

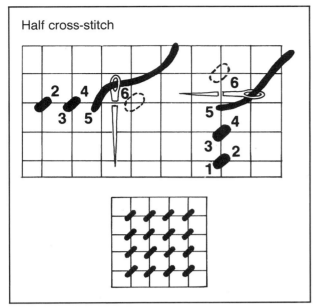

Straight gobelin stitch

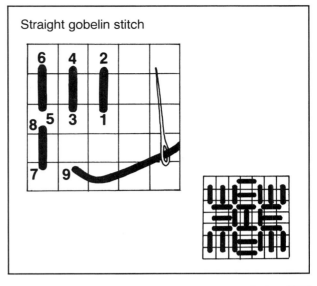

Mosaic stitch

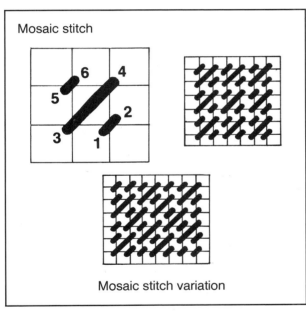

Mosaic stitch variation

Tent stitch

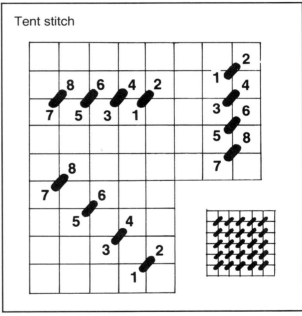

Slanting gobelin stitch

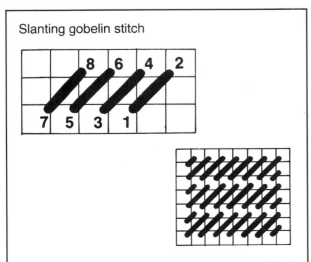

Triple cross-stitch

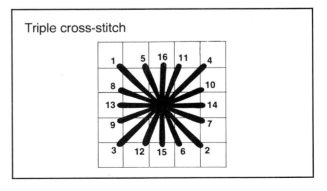

Design and Photography Credits

Designs

We would like to extend our heartfelt thanks and appreciation to the craft designers who contributed ideas, designs, and projects to our book.

David Ashe—hat rack and coat-rack, animals, belt buckles, rowboat, 34; napkin rings, necklace, fish plaque, wooden toys, 37; puzzle, 58; mosaic, 59; desk top organizer, 184

John Baker—cook book, 9

Devora Belilove—paper-covered boxes, 28

Gary Boling—wall hanging, 21; man's jacket, 94; girl's jacket, 109; afghan, 182

Jackie Curry—sheep, 140

Mark Davis—wooden toys, 154-155

Deborah Dugan—lace collar, 98

Phyllis Dunstan—pillows, 11; paper projects, 28; cards, 46; collar, 99; shirts, 102; party hats, centerpiece, 136-137; spoon dolls, 141; doll furniture, 142-143; toy soldier doll, 147; bandanna doll, 148; sponge toys, 156; train, 158; dollhouse, 160-161

Sandra Elser-Ciminero—bedspread, 125

Linda Emmerson—frames, 61; space station, 159

Dixie Falls—afghan, 183

Ann and Amy Finch—portraits, 124

Viviana Frigerio—dolls, 138-139

Pat Gaska—backpacks, 88

Diane Gilman—skirt, 93

Flavin Glover—tablecloth, 169

Janet Harrington—collages, 63; shirts, hats, 100; roses, 194; geometric paper trims, 205

Linda Hicks—puzzles, 157

Laura Holtorf—samplers, 42; woman's jacket, 94; sampler, 162-163

Ray Holtorf—leather bags, 39

Corabelle Hutcheson—vest, 96

Impressions—cupid pillows, 60

Adam, Amy, and Rebecca Jerdee—printing workshop projects, 200-203

Photographs

Many thanks, as well, to the photographers who contributed their creative energy and technical skills to this book.

Mike Dieter—13, 17, 21, 24-25, 39, 59, 84, 88, 95, 113, 126, 127, 129, 138-139, 157, 167, 169, 170, 172, 180, 182, 183, 185, 188, 204, 205

Jim Hedrich, for Hedrich-Blessing—19, 109, 121

Thomas Hooper—9, 10, 34, 37, 40, 46, 54, 55, 58, 93, 100, 102, 104, 111, 140, 142, 148, 154, 155, 184, 186, 187

William N. Hopkins—Cover, 6-7, 11, 15, 16, 23, 27, 30-31, 42, 47, 48-49, 51, 53, 60, 61, 80, 81, 82, 83, 99, 116-117, 118, 119, 130, 131, 132, 133, 134, 135, 141, 152, 153, 156, 158, 166, 170, 171, 172, 173, 177, 178, 181, 184, 198, 199, 200, 201, 202, 203, 207

Index

Index